Joys of the Not So Perfect Woman

*Stories of
Holy Awareness Moments
with a Perfect God*

ARLETTE REVELLS

Joys of the Not So Perfect Woman

 Published by Great Works Creation Co.
Athens, Georgia 30605
www.greatworksinc.com

Copyright © 2024 by Arlette Revells

All rights reserved. No part of this publication may be reproduced, distributed or transmitted in any form or by any means, including photocopying, recording, or other electronic or mechanical methods, without the prior written permission from the author or her agents, except in the case of brief quotations embodied in reviews and certain other noncommercial uses permitted by copyright law.

Adherence to all applicable laws and regulations, including international, federal, state, and local governing professional licensing, business practices, advertising, and all other aspects of doing business in the US, Canada, or any other jurisdiction is the sole responsibility of the purchaser or reader.

Any perceived slight of any individual or organization is purely unintentional.

Unless otherwise noted, all Scripture quotations are from THE HOLY BIBLE, NEW INTERNATIONAL VERSION®, NIV® Copyright © 1973, 1978, 1984, 2011 by Biblica, Inc.® Used by permission. All rights reserved worldwide.

Scripture taken from the New King James Version®, NKJV®. Copyright © 1982 by Thomas Nelson. Used by permission. All rights reserved.

Scripture quotations marked NLT are taken from the Holy Bible, New Living Translation, copyright © 1996, 2004, 2015 by Tyndale House Foundation. Used by permission of Tyndale House Publishers, Inc., Carol Stream, Illinois 60188. All rights reserved.

Cover and Interior Design by Great Works Creation Co.

ISBN: 979-8-9905102-0-3 (paperback)
ISBN: 979-8-9905102-2-7 (hardback)
ISBN: 979-8-9905102-1-0 (eBook)

Produced and Printed in the United States of America

— **Barbara James,** President, Joysprings Foundation, Inc.

"Arlette is a multi-talented person, a creative and articulate communicator, who knows how to bring 'sparkle' to life experiences amid the 'musical blend' of truth and wisdom. She shares profound truths in beautifully dramatic expressions that will cause you to engage new levels of personal transformation from the heart!"

— **Arlene Bridges Samuels,** Weekly Featured Columnist for The Christian Broadcasting Network Israel

"Rare is the writer who blends humor and inspiration into her personal stories. My treasured friend Arlette is among them. Reading each story is to embrace a blessing. Fill your heart with laughter—and your mind—with challenges wrapped in soft cashmere words to deepen your faith."

— **Christine Wyrtzen,** Founder, Daughters of Promise

"I remember the first time Arlette told me one of her God-stories. I didn't move through the entire thing. I was captivated and hardly took a breath. That's because stories teach us. That's why Jesus told so many of them. He knew that they take us to the heart of God. Defenses are down when our imagination is engaged. Such is the nature of this book. Arlette takes us on an adventure by sharing some unforgettable and inspiring stories. When we get to the last page, we will realize that our perceptions and perspectives have changed because she looked through the lens of eternity with artist's eyes and told us what she saw. This woman is a rare jewel. You will trace the countenance of the Spirit when reading Arlette's God-encounters."

— J. Lee Grady
Author and Director of The Mordecai Project

"When I met Arlette Revells years ago, I was amazed by her infectious joy. Her joy is not based on moods, circumstances or people. She has learned the secret of true joy, and I'm so glad she is sharing that secret in this special book. The stories of her spiritual journey will encourage you, build your faith and prompt lots of laughter, which is the best medicine!"

— Dr. Chuck D. Pierce
President of Glory of Zion International,
Kingdom Harvest Alliance

"In all my journeys around the world, two of the most incredible people the Lord has brought into my life are Arlette and Lavon Revells. In the early days, we would have prayer retreats and go to Gatlinburg, Tennessee. Arlette was very spiritual but learning to follow the Spirit of God. As the Lord revealed Himself to her, she would share some of the most incredible testimonies—many of which you will find in *Joys of the Not So Perfect Woman: Stories of Holy Awareness Moments with a Perfect God*. This book has some of the most delightful stories you will ever read. From the Lord teaching her that He could "dress" her for the future, bringing her victory out of failure, facing her fears, and keeping her joy throughout the journey, you will experience faith on each page. This book is a JOY to read!"

Dedication & Thank You!

This book is dedicated to my incredible husband, Lavon Revells. You've always been my "knight in shining armor," especially when you rescued me from that giant snake in the garage. The unwavering support you extended during the writing of this book exceeded what I could have imagined. Truly, I couldn't have done this without you. Sharing my journey on Earth with you, my forever boyfriend, is a gift from God. I'm so grateful that He brought us together! Brace yourself; there's much more to come!

My heartfelt thanks go to you, my children, Laura and Christopher, for your support during this monumental journey. Your prayers and encouragement have been a significant source of strength and inspiration. (Thank you, Laura, for the many hours of late-night help. It took both of us to "birth" this book on time.) Knowing that my husband, children, and grandchildren share in the joy of their own holy awareness moments fills my heart with joy.

I extend a huge thanks to my friends who spent many hours contributing to the completion of this project. I will forever be grateful to you.

And...thank you, everyone, for your prayer support.

A big thank you to the women who shared their
stories and poem in this volume of
*Joys of the Not So Perfect Woman: Stories of Holy Awareness
Moments with a Perfect God.*

*My sheep listen to my voice;
I know them, and they follow me.*
(John 10:27)

Contents

STORY 1	Make Me Look Good, Please!	11
	The Joy of Inner Beauty	
STORY 2	Two Dolls, One Huge Lesson	17
	The Joy of Perfect Love	
STORY 3	The Confirmation Dress	21
	The Joy of the Ultimate Beauty Secret	
STORY 4	The Mask	35
	The Joy of Being Unique	
STORY 5	Bees and Roses	41
	The Joy of the Ageless	
STORY 6	The Fight to Breathe	55
	The Joy of the Little Green Bag	
STORY 7	Onward to the Nursery	67
	The Joy Gift	
STORY 8	Get up! Throw Out the Line	73
	The Joy of Redeemed Time	
STORY 9	Stomach in, Sternum high, and Shoulders back!	81
	Joy in the Face of Fear:	
	Passing the Baton of Confidence	
STORY 10	Love Story, Part 1:	91
	The Joy of becoming Victorious after Failure	
	Love Story, Part 2:	95
	The Joy of God's Love Story	
	Epilogue	105
	Photos	106
	About the Author	108

*Show me your ways, Lord,
teach me your paths.*
(Psalm 25:4)

Holy Awareness Moments

LIFE EVENTS THAT CAN ONLY BE ARRANGED BY GOD

As you "journey" through this book, you will read a series of true stories, places in time where "holy awareness moments" occurred in the lives of ordinary people like you and me.

Join me, a not-so-perfect woman, as we "travel" together through some of my stories and those of some other women. These are the stories where God showed up in our lives in a very real and tangible way. In these holy awareness moments, we become aware of and experience the presence of our perfect God as "He works all things together for our good." These moments confirm that God is real, that He cares, and that He is present in every little detail of our lives, just as He is in yours.

I believe God's desire is to increase our spiritual intuition, guiding us to explore and discern the map of our life experiences. He wants us to see His heart more clearly and to also discover evidence of His boundless love for us. Are you ready to begin our thrilling adventure of self-discovery and spiritual growth?

As you begin this journey with me, may you discover moments of holy awareness—gentle embraces from your loving Father. My prayer is that my stories stir your heart to share your own with courage and joy. For it is in our stories that others are drawn to travel the path with us and awaken to their own sacred moments of transformation.

Arlette

STORY 1
Make Me Look Good, Please!
The Joy of Inner Beauty

In my quest for physical perfection, I found a treasure: a pair of foam rubber shoulder pads that promised a new silhouette! I carefully placed a pad on each shoulder when I dressed for church the following Sunday morning. That was back in the day when big shoulder pads were in style. For me, the logic was simple: large shoulder pads meant broader shoulders and a miraculously smaller waist—a silhouette any woman might want.

Picture this: the church service ended, and George, a long-time family friend, greeted me with his deep, low voice that resonates from the depths of his very being. "Good morning," he said.

I responded, "Hi, George. How are you today?"

His response came with a bonus feature—a slight wince with a quick backward jerk of his head as he looked down toward the floor. *Oh no, did something fall on the floor?* I wondered. *What was so captivating?* I took a look.

At first, I didn't recognize it, and then I realized what it was. It was one of my shoulder pads! The shapely foam rubber shoulder pad on the green carpet looked like an intimate part of my body.

Mortified and with as much dignity as possible, I stooped to pick it up. It was bigger than my hand. I quickly squeezed it tightly as I stood back up, wishing it would disappear.

George's raised eyebrows and perplexed look told me he still wondered what it was. As matter-of-fact as possible, I said, "Oh, that's one of my shoulder pads."

George gave his throat a little "ahem" and awkwardly said, "I wondered...where that came from."

~~~

PRESSING ON

Nevertheless, undeterred by the awkward moment, I pressed on in my quest for perfection. In addition to that pursuit, other accounts of personal awkward moments found their place within my collection of "make me look good" stories. Often, they serve me well when I have to navigate uneasy social situations.

~~~

BRIDAL SHOWER LUNCHEON

A few years down the road, I received an invitation to a bridal shower luncheon. Arriving, I was the last to be seated at a round table surrounded by friendly, elegantly dressed women I did not know. In my eyes, they all seemed to wear the crown of the "Perfect Woman." Everyone appeared to be friends already, chatting easily—everyone except me. I felt invisible. However, the situation was okay, as I found listening to their conversation entertaining.

Suddenly, one of the women looked at me, causing a hush to fall over the group as they, too, turned their attention

STORY 1: Make Me Look Good, Please!

towards me. I don't know if the first lady thought I had attempted to join in or if she just wanted me to feel included in their wedding stories.

What do you say when a table of "perfect crown" women waits for you to speak? My forced contribution to the wedding chatter paved the way for me to head to my story-telling comfort zone. A perfect story bounced into my thoughts from my collection of personal "make me look good" stories. My story began:

> After a few years of owning a business specializing in visual communications, I expanded my services by adding an online wedding invitation store. (Perhaps being at a bridal shower luncheon brought this story to mind.)
>
> I wanted to create a website that evokes the warmth of personal care as if the brides met face-to-face with a knowledgeable wedding consultant at a local store.
>
> Making an appointment with the best photographer in town, I described my plan, saying, "I need the perfect 'welcoming' photo. Make me look good, please!" He patiently waited while I changed my outfits several times and experimented with different hairstyles. Over an hour later, he completed his photography session.
>
> Within a week, he sent me the pictures to review digitally. I selected an image of me standing behind a desk in my navy blue business suit. I flashed a big smile that signaled, "Hi, thank you for visiting my online store."
>
> After carefully studying my picture over the next few days, my designer's perspective whispered, "It isn't enough." I decided I might look better if

I removed a bit of width around the hipline. As a graphic design artist, I could easily make that happen. I reshaped, tucked, and nipped my digital self. I took off twenty pounds within seconds! I enjoyed the fast results with the most manageable "diet plan" ever: Digital weight loss!

Not long after going public with my new website, the telephone rang. The voice of a good friend, whom I had seen a few days earlier, greeted me. With her southern charm, she exclaimed, "Arlette, I just wanted to call and let you know that I checked out your new website, and you look wonderful. I believe you've lost weight."

I didn't tell her my little secret. But, if she had looked closer, she would have noticed what I had done. My shadow was cast onto the desk and did not match my new slim self!

Arlette Revells (note the shadow on the desk)

Laughter erupted from the women around the table listening to my story. A sense of delight fueled my boundless enthusiasm for sharing stories.

HOLY AWARENESS MOMENT

One day, after a satisfying workout at the gym, I decided to relax my muscles by soaking in the swirling whirlpool water in the aquatic area. A few other women had the same idea and were already there.

Among them was a newcomer with striking outward beauty, but unfortunately, she lost her charm as soon as she started talking. Her angry and cynical words revealed her inner turmoil, making her beauty appear superficial. I recognized her inner turmoil from the words she spoke: Self-discontent.

Self-discontent has the potential to fester if we compare ourselves to the cultural values around us (Romans 12:2), showcasing the difference between superficial and inner beauty.

Scripture tells us, "If anyone is in Christ, the new creation has come: The old has gone, the new is here (2 Corinthians 5:17)!"

True beauty emanates from the inside out. It's a supernatural beauty glowing from within. It is profound and can't be copied. ~

Am I beautiful?

By Victoria Allen

The flowers are beautiful, each one adorned with a unique array of colors, each petal displaying its singular beauty.

The sun is beautiful—hiding each night to arise in full glory the next day. You cannot escape it. Even when you aren't looking at it, its glow radiates the day.

The moon is beautiful. Its humility in the night sky provides just enough light while still giving the night its proper due job of letting me sleep and rest for the next day.

The stars are beautiful. Each one is placed exactly where it's supposed to be. They share in their twinkling of beauty, and all together they form something worth awe.

JOYS OF THE NOT SO PERFECT WOMAN ...

The birds are beautiful. Look at how their feathers flutter and fly in the sky in varying colors and shapes. Some fly in groups, and others are perfectly content by themselves.

The trees are beautiful. The way their leaves sway in the wind, change colors, and come to life in the spring after a long winter, let me know that there is always a new beginning in time.

The mountains are beautiful. They are so big, and I feel so tiny next to them, but the view at the top gives me a new perspective and appreciation for all that's before me. Suddenly, my own worries and fears disappear.

None of these things ask for attention, yet their beauty screams. It is evident in their essence—it's just what they are!

If all of these things are beautiful, how much more precious am I in my loving Father's eyes?

What does my Father say about me? You are all together beautiful, my darling; there is no flaw in you.

He clothes me in strength and dignity, and I can laugh in the days to come.

I praise God because I am fearfully and wonderfully made; His works are wonderful; I know that full well.

Yes—I am beautiful too.

Let the beauty of the Lord our God be upon us, And establish the work of our hands for us.
(Psalm 90:17 NKJV)

STORY 2
Two Dolls, One Huge Lesson
The Joy of Perfect Love

A friend, Jim, introduced me to Christine Wyrtzen a few years ago. He felt we had a lot in common. Jim was right. We became spiritual sisters right away. Christine and I lived just minutes apart for many years, yet we never crossed paths until Jim introduced us. It's a testament to how unexpected and beautiful surprises can come from even the closest corners of our lives. Our friendship is one such example.

As we sip our coffee, Christine and I enjoy sharing stories about how God has touched the deepest parts of our hearts through everyday life events. One of these powerful stories is Christine's doll story, which left a lasting impression on me.

CHRISTINE'S DOLL STORY:
Many years back, Christine was the guest performer at a church in Wisconsin. Before the concert, she had been sent

to change her clothes in the church nursery since there was an adjoining private bathroom.

She said, "I was dressed earlier than expected and had time to kill, so I roamed the nursery looking at the toys scattered around the room. In the corner was a doll lying on the floor. She was face down, naked, and in rough shape from all the years of rough handling. Her hair was matted, and there were numerous scuff marks over her body. I picked her up, looked at her for a long minute, and said to her out loud, 'I know you. I feel like you tonight.'"

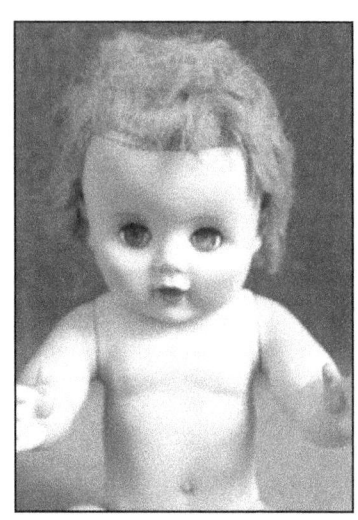

Hope

Christine continued, "Sounds funny to say, but I was not trying to be humorous at the time. I was tired, disillusioned with ministry, and felt that the person who would be taking the stage was not the person I thought I was on the inside. It's hard to believe that this doll was once new in a box. She was a gift that lit up some young girl's face. But that was long ago. Now, she's been around the block a few times and has gotten pretty streetwise."

She continued, "Sometime later, the church was kind enough to give me the doll. I realized that I felt like that doll each time I pictured being alone with God. I couldn't imagine Him looking at me with perfect love and acceptance."

"Tragically," she continued, "this is how many, and probably most, see themselves. Looking up into God's face and keeping eye contact seems frightening."

At the birth of a new ministry, **Daughters of Promise**, she said that God was doing a lot of deep work in her soul.

STORY 2: Two Dolls, One Huge Lesson

Jule

She decided that she needed a new representation of who she was in Christ. *How about a new doll*, came to her thoughts.

THE NEW DOLL

Christine continued, "Not really being a doll person, per se, I was intrigued to go to a doll collector's store. In the store window was a doll sitting in a white, wicker rocking chair. She wore a white eyelet lace dress, and her blond hair spilled beautifully over her shoulders. I was quite taken and asked the store owner if he could get her out of the display so I could see her."

Christine noticed a nametag hanging from the doll's wrist that read, "Jule." The back of the tag explained her origin, that she had been hand-made by a German artist who was well known for her creation of lifelike hands and feet.

Christine shared, "What captivated me most about Jule, though she was exquisite in every way, was her eyes. They looked so real and seemed to gaze right through you."

Christine purchased the doll that day and thought her name appropriate, Jule—the apple of God's eyes.

"Jule and the naked doll (I named her Hope) are in my home now," Christine said, "For years, they sat side by side in my office. They represented how I used to see myself and who I came to understand that I am. For a long time, this was the end of this story."

THE TWIST

"But, there's now a twist," Christine continued, "I paid many hundreds of dollars for Jule, so I was very careful when I traveled with her. I taped her eyelashes down so that they wouldn't break. I braided her hair so it wouldn't get knotted. I wrapped her in bubble wrap and then wrapped her again in an Amish-made baby quilt. And when I went to pack the naked doll, I just threw her in the suitcase. I figured, "How could she be any more damaged!"

"But after an event," Christine explained, "An experienced doll collector asked me if she could see the naked doll. After examining her, she informed me that she was valuable. Worth a couple thousand dollars.

"After recovering from the shock," Christine said, "I realized I had been bubble-wrapping the wrong doll!"

HOLY AWARENESS MOMENT
"The next time I looked at Hope, the naked doll," Christine shared, "I realized that THIS is the one Jesus comes to put His arms around. THIS is the one to whom He says, *"I have called you and you are Mine. Though the mountains may tremble and the hills may be shaken, my covenant of love with you will never go away. I have you inscribed on the palms of my hands."* ~

But God demonstrates His own love for us in this: While we were still sinners, Christ died for us.
(Romans 5:8)

STORY 3

The Confirmation Dress

The Joy of the Ultimate Beauty Secret

I know what you might think when you read this story. I would wonder the same thing, yet the following story really happened.

THE DIVINE MESSENGER
I was tired and desperate to fall asleep on a late Friday night, June 7, 1985. Crawling into my comfortable bed, I realized I had neglected to set the alarm clock on the dresser. My routine for some time was to get up at 4:00 a.m. for my quiet time with God. As I drifted to sleep, I mumbled, "God, if You need me to get up early in the morning, help me wake up."

I was sleeping on my back when I became aware of a beautiful, larger-than-life heavenly being leaning over me with flowing robes, like dancing white energy. I knew it was an angel. I heard these words: "Get up; I have something for you this morning." The angel then disappeared. I quickly slipped from under the covers, careful not to awaken my husband. It was 4:23 a.m.

Adrenaline running high, I tiptoed down the hall, trying to keep the hardwood floors from creaking. I didn't want to awaken our two children: Laura, who had graduated from high school the night before, and Christopher, our tenth grader. My mother-in-law, visiting from South Georgia for Laura's graduation, was sleeping in another bedroom across the hall.

FIRST INSTRUCTION

Wonder seized my imagination. I knew that what was happening was bigger than me. After all, I had asked God to awaken me if necessary! Think about it. An angel was sent to wake me up with a message! I knew it had to be important.

I grabbed my Bible from the den on my way to the kitchen. Sitting at the kitchen table, I started turning pages haphazardly. As I did, I heard these words in my spirit, "From this day forward, I shall supply your clothes My way. I will provide for all your needs. You shall be able to buy clothes for others, but I shall supply your clothes through others."

Stunned, I sat there thinking about what I had heard. I knew that the words were from God; I would *never* have thought of such things myself.

Disappointment consumed me. I loved buying clothes. My motto was and is: Take the time to look your best; it breeds success. Looking back on that experience, I now know why God sent a special messenger: He knew I would need a sign from Heaven. Little did I suspect how it would come and what it would be.

The biblical story of Gideon came to mind. One day, he was minding his own business, threshing wheat, when God appeared and commissioned him to save Israel. Poor

STORY 3: The Confirmation Dress

Gideon pleaded and protested, saying, "How can I save Israel? My clan is the weakest in Manasseh, and I am the least in my family."

When the angel first appeared to Gideon that day, the angel addressed Gideon with, "The Lord is with you, mighty warrior." Gideon felt like anything but a mighty warrior. At the time, he was hiding from the Midianites, trying to thresh his grain without being killed. God saw in Gideon what he could become: a mighty warrior. But Gideon didn't see himself as a mighty anything. God continued speaking, "Go and save Israel out of Midian's hand. Am I not sending you?" God assured Gideon that He would be with him.

I'm sure Gideon had no idea what was lined up for him when he got out of bed that day! (Like me as I sat at my kitchen table dazed and expectant.) If you want to read this fascinating story about Gideon, it's in Judges chapter 6.

No one asked me to save a nation that morning, but God announced that He was taking charge of my clothes! "Save a nation" might have been more exciting and doable than the words He gave me. After all, I loved clothes.

I was still sitting at the kitchen table when I decided to "put out a fleece." Gideon did it. Here's how it unfolded for him.

He asked God for a sign saying, "If you will save Israel by my hand as you have promised—look, I will place a wool fleece on the threshing floor. If there is dew only on the fleece and all the ground is dry, then I will know that you will save Israel by my hand, as you said."

Gideon rose early the next day; he squeezed the fleece and wrung out the dew—filling a bowlful of water, yet the ground was dry. Wanting more proof, Gideon then pleaded with God, "Do not be angry with me. I have one more request. Allow me one more test with the fleece. This time, make the fleece dry and the ground covered with dew." That night, God did so; the ground was covered with dew, but the fleece, and only the fleece, was dry.

THE FLEECE

I concluded from this story that a fleece would be permitted. I decided to negotiate, too! My fleece was simple: "Lord, if this is really You telling me I can't buy my clothes anymore, please give me a confirmation dress today through someone." In a sense, I rubbed my "spiritual hands" together, left the matter in my Father's hands, and breathed a sigh of relief. That took care of it. Surely, if God wanted to do something supernatural with my clothes, He would respond to my fleece. And then I would have no questions.

Lavon and I had planned to take his mother on a scenic 75-mile trip to Helen, Georgia, that day, a trip he and I had enjoyed many times before. After breakfast, we headed to the car. I quickly volunteered to sit in the back seat so I could snuggle into my thoughts about everything that had happened that morning. *Will I get my confirmation dress today*? I wondered.

I didn't mention my early morning experience to Lavon or his mother. After all, my morning experience with God was still new, fragile, and tenuous.

Traveling amid the stunning scenery between Athens and Helen, my thoughts were so engaged in my early morning experience that the beautiful scenery and the Alpine shopping village, nestled in the North Georgia mountains, didn't distract me. In my thoughts, I kept repeating the words I had heard from God earlier. Part of me continued to wrestle in discomfort, while another part of me felt strangely "warm."

During the drive, my mind raced, searching for scriptures to confirm my early morning experience. I knew that if the message were indeed from God, there would be scripture to support it. As I pondered, a verse soon came to mind:

STORY 3: The Confirmation Dress

"And why do you worry about clothes? See how the lilies of the field grow? They do not labor or spin. Yet I tell you that not even Solomon in all his splendor was dressed like one of these. If that is how God clothes the grass of the field, which is here today and tomorrow is thrown into the fire, will He not much more clothe you, O you of little faith? So do not worry, saying, 'What shall we eat?' or 'What shall we drink?' or 'What shall we wear?'" (Matthew 6:28-31)

I wondered, "Is God going to clothe me as He does the lilies of the field?" I was counting on His response to my fleece.

DISAPPOINTMENT BECAME EXPECTANCY
By the time we arrived in Helen, a significant attitude shift had occurred within me. Disappointment became expectancy. Only God could have done that so quickly, literally within hours.

The day slowly passed as I walked in and out of the clothing shops. If this were the place where God intended to respond to my fleece, He would indeed speak to one of the shop owners about a lady to whom they should give a dress that day.

I watched for some shop owner to lean out of their door and proclaim, "It's you! I know it! You're the one I'm supposed to give a dress to." I knew God was capable of doing that. I felt so "warm" that I wondered if there was a glow about me. After all, I had been in the presence of an angel, and I believed I had just heard from God! No one offered me a confirmation dress while in Helen.

Returning home, I opted for the back seat again.

While I was sure I had heard from God, I was now afraid I wouldn't get the confirmation dress. I wondered, "How will God deliver the dress to me today? After all, my fleece, my confirmation-dress-request, specified that I would receive the dress today." Time was running out.

Then, it suddenly dawned on me: "Maybe He will give me my dress through Mother!" She was helping at the church garage sale that day and was always on the lookout for beautiful clothes. I convinced myself that Mother must have found a dress for me and had it delivered while we were gone. I strained to see if a dress was hanging at the back door as we pulled into the garage. Nope, no dress. As soon as we stepped inside the house, I called Mother.

"Hi, Mother, we're back home. How was your day? How did the church sale go?" She never mentioned a dress for me when she told me about her day.

UNEXPECTED RESPONSE TO MY FLEECE
Bedtime was coming fast. No dress had appeared. "Was it all my imagination? God, I don't understand." Then, His still, small voice spoke to me, "Your fleece was contrary to what I said. I will supply your clothes My way, and that includes My timing." It was comforting to hear His voice again. I felt settled and no longer anxious. I would wait for God to unveil the next part of this unusual journey.

OVERFLOWING CLOSET
I reasoned that not being able to buy more new clothes wouldn't be so bad. My closets overflowed with beautiful things. I loved the description of how the Proverbs 31 woman dressed like royalty in gowns of the finest cloth. One Bible translation described her clothing as silk and purple. *I love silk dresses too*, I thought, *and I've got enough clothes to wear for the rest of my life if I don't gain too much weight.*

STORY 3: The Confirmation Dress

SECOND INSTRUCTION

However, a few days later, God spoke to me again, "I want you to give away every piece of clothing you have, all the pieces of clothing that you picked out." Things were getting a little more serious now. God was asking me to trust Him to supply my clothes and to give away all the clothes I had to do with selecting! Was this a reverse fleece? Was God asking me for a sign that I trusted Him?

By then, that "warm" feeling had engulfed me so much that I knew something heavenly was happening. I wanted to be part of it. Joy and a sense of adventure joined my growing expectancy. "Okay, Lord. I'm willing. I will trust You to show me to whom I'm supposed to give my clothes."

"MINOR" ISSUE

How will I tell my husband that I am to give away all my clothes? Although frugal, Lavon was always very generous regarding my clothes. He often insisted on adding to my wardrobe for every special occasion. He knew his gifts always delighted me, especially boutique clothes! He would usually involve me in the shopping so I could choose what I loved.

How would I tell him I was giving away all those nice clothes? But God had been very specific about the clothes I should give away. They were to be the ones I had chosen for myself.

The day came when I finally told Lavon. We had just enjoyed lunch together and sat in the car outside the office building where I worked. I still didn't understand everything, but by then, I felt a sense of specialness—not an arrogant specialness, but a humble recognition that God had stepped into my life for a particular purpose. I found myself in a place of holy mystery. Sitting next to Lavon, I wondered how to express everything that had happened with adequate language. Struggling to control my emotions, I blurted out,

"God has asked me to give away my clothes. Not only that, but I can no longer buy or select any new clothes for myself. He said that He will supply my clothes through others."

A visible sense of relief swept over his face as he said, "I knew something had been happening but was afraid to ask. I was waiting for you to tell me when you were ready." I'm not sure which was the source of more relief to him: that I would no longer be buying clothes for myself or that I wasn't concealing the news of a potentially severe illness from him.

THE GIVEAWAY

In response to my new instructions to give away every piece of clothing I had any part in choosing, I took an inventory of my closets. I found only three pieces I had not picked: a blouse and two skirts! I had never worn them because they were not "me." I couldn't remember who had kindly passed them along, but I was glad they had! They were the only clothes that would remain in my closet after everything else was given away.

The giveaway plan started emerging. To begin with, I was to give specific clothes to specific individuals. Excitedly, I began to prepare my clothes, my gift offerings, for the moments when God would tell me the recipients. Each piece of clothing now represented a gift I hoped someone would treasure, but at the same time, each was also an offering to God. It felt like I was preparing gifts for Christmas, something I've always enjoyed doing.

A CLOTHING FUNERAL

The moment arrived when I began preparing my very favorite dress as a gift offering. That evening, I placed it in the washing machine and suddenly realized I had worn it for the last time. Warm tears began to flow down my cheeks, and memories of moments and places I had worn the dress washed over me.

STORY 3: The Confirmation Dress

As I prepared to have each subsequent piece of clothing cleaned, I knew something important was happening deep inside. Each garment was somehow representative of my inner journey. It wasn't about my attachment to the clothes themselves. Each item symbolized a fragment of myself that I was holding onto. God was tenderly addressing each one, ever the patient teacher.

My teenage children, Laura and Christopher, watched me leave the laundry room. Something had happened. My eyes were red from crying. They asked, "Mom, what just happened in there?" I assured them everything was all right and that I had been praying. I didn't tell them the long story, or mention the process of saying goodbye to my clothes, including my favorite dress.

THIRD INSTRUCTION

Nine days after I received my instruction to give away my clothes, I realized that another part of me was coming to life. A realignment was taking place. God spoke to me again early that morning: "Today is the day you are to start wearing only those clothes you had nothing to do with picking out." The test was getting steep, and it was deeply personal. I was trying to assimilate the meaning of it all.

HOLY AWARENESS MOMENT

At this point, I still had a closet full of nice clothes, but I could no longer wear them. I dressed for work, putting on the blouse and one of the two skirts someone had given to me. What was once not "my style" was now all I had. Somehow, it didn't seem to matter as much as I thought it would. I was grateful for the blouse and two skirts.

A surprise greeted me when I turned to check myself in the large mirror in the powder room. It was as if I saw my reflection in a divine mirror. I smiled. Inner beauty smiled back at me, revealing a deeper, more beautiful version of myself. God was letting me see myself through His eyes; it was eye-opening and humbling.

While God was providing clothes for my body, the part of me that interacts with the physical world, He was also adorning my spirit, the innermost part of me that connects with Him. A reflection of love, joy, and peace adorned the new radiant woman I had never seen before, the one I was getting to know. She looked royal and confident—a stark change from my previous perception. God was showing me the person He sees, the person He saw long ago when He created me, revealing a beauty far more incredible than I had imagined.

That was the first surprise of the day. Another surprise was yet to come!

ANOTHER SURPRISE

After I came home from work that day, I heard someone coming through the back door. Our daughter, Laura, entered the kitchen where I was preparing dinner. She held a beautifully gift-wrapped package in her arms, placed it on the counter, and excitedly announced, "God asked me to buy this for you."

Amazed, I quickly removed the ribbons and wrapping paper and lifted the top off the box. Nestled underneath the crisp pink tissue paper was a beautiful pink silk dress! The moment was surreal. Then, I realized: **This is God's confirmation dress, my sign!** I knew it had to be God because no one knew what He had asked me to do that morning.

"Mother," Laura said excitedly, "Today, when I got my paycheck, all I could think about was surprising you with a new dress!" It was her very first summer job and her very first paycheck.

I danced around, laughed, and grabbed Laura with a big

STORY 3: The Confirmation Dress

hug. God was hugging me through her! God had reduced and expanded my dress choices—all on the same day!

THE FREE BOUTIQUE

Though many days had passed, some clothes remained in my closet that I had not given away. So, I set aside an evening to gather them and complete God's assignment. (I was to give away every piece of clothing I had previously picked out.)

The big clothes giveaway time arrived. I invited my mother, sister, and two sisters-in-law to my house for this event. They had no idea why I asked them over. I lovingly displayed my clothes in our living room and dining room. Clothes were everywhere. Some were on hangers hooked over door facings. Others were draped over chairs and furniture, along with all the accessories.

Everyone entered the kitchen door from the garage. I had closed the living and dining room doors so they couldn't see the department store in the adjoining rooms. First, I wanted to share with them what God was doing in my life, and I didn't want the sight of the clothes to distract them.

Finally, I opened my "Free Boutique" and asked them to "shop" and take everything home with them: all the clothes they could wear and those they thought someone else could wear. I'll never forget how solemn and shy they were. After much encouragement from me, they hesitantly started "shopping." I overheard one of my sisters-in-law whisper, "This is like being at a funeral." She had no clue how true her statement was. They took most of the clothes with them that night, and I gave the rest to a local charity.

Mother called a few days later. "Honey," she said, "I want to take you shopping for a new dress. I need you to show me what you want, and I will pay for it."

"I'll be glad to go shopping with you, Mother, and I will try on anything you pick out for me. But you must be the one to select the clothes you want me to try on. You must also be the one to decide what you want to buy for me. God has been clear with His instructions. I cannot buy clothes for myself, and I can't even pick out anything someone else wants to buy for me." She agreed. I then modeled for Mother the clothes she chose.

GRADUATION
Since God did not change His instructions for a while, I wondered if I would ever go shopping again and pick out clothes for myself. As far as I knew, God had ordained a life-long faith walk of trusting Him in this area.

But after three and a half years of wearing what others had selected and given to me, God spoke again about my wardrobe. When folding the family laundry one day, I picked up one of my husband's oversized T-shirts to fold. I used to love to wear it around the house. As I folded it these words came into my thoughts, "You can wear that shirt if you want."

"Oh, no," I resisted, thinking it was a temptation. Then, I quickly realized God was releasing me to select and purchase my clothes again. My interesting "graduation dress" was Lavon's T-shirt!

THE ULTIMATE BEAUTY SECRET
My long-time life's motto: Take the time to look your best; it breeds success, still reverberates through my being, but now it starts in my spiritual "closet." I still have my "sense of style," woven into me in my mother's womb. However, my physical wardrobe no longer takes precedence over spiritual adornments. I open the Bible daily and step into God's world—where I am encouraged to clothe myself in what is pure and lovely, finally slipping into the shoes of the kingdom.

There, I shed the garments of what is carnal, the tattered

STORY 3: The Confirmation Dress

rags of this world, by confessing and asking for forgiveness of my sins. Then, I step into the exquisite garments of the redeemed. Those beautiful garments are adorned with dignity, confidence, strength, joy, praise, hope, and worship. The selection is "out of this world!" Dressed in God's finest, I am equipped better to handle the difficulties and challenges of life on Earth.

During my journey with clothing, God redefined beauty for me. True beauty, as He revealed, transcends age, ability, and time—it's a loveliness clothed in strength and dignity and woven with the glory of God. I can say with all my heart, THIS is the ultimate beauty secret!

MORE ...

Have you ever considered the incredible hidden beauty of creation that no one sees except God? He created everything beautiful for His enjoyment. How much more did He, the Creator of the lovely "lilies of the field" take delight in creating you and me?

He fashioned us for the purpose of a relationship with Him. A relationship with Him is a choice, not a demand. I recently heard that God gave us the power to *choose* to love Him because it adds value to our love. How special is that?

My spiritual wardrobe didn't just change; I underwent a complete shift in my perception of myself. This transformation was guided by Holy Spirit, living within my spirit. (1 Corinthians 6:19-20).

Just as Queen Esther was prepared to be the bride of King Xerxes, we are being prepared by Holy Spirit because we are the bride of Christ. He purifies us, then adorns us in robes of righteousness, preparing us for the glorious return of our mighty Groom, King Jesus, the Son of God. Can you imagine the splendor of that wedding?

Our Bridegroom is eager and anxious for the reunion.

He turns to His Father, perhaps each hour, asking if it's time yet to bring us home. I don't want to be caught unprepared. Each morning as I dress, I am ever more conscious of what's most important: eternal garments. ~

Strength and honor are her clothing;
She shall rejoice in time to come.
(Proverbs 31:25a NKJV)

STORY 4

The Mask

The Joy of Being Unique

The sound of the piano echoed through our living room. My parents bought it for me when my mother insisted it was time for me to start taking lessons. Although she longed to play herself, she never had formal training.

Despite her unfulfilled dream, she mastered one chord, effortlessly playing it up and down the keyboard in different octaves. Whenever that chord sounded, I hurried to the living room to witness it. Her posture exuded confidence and grace.

Finally, the piano lessons began. Mother made sure her "little princess" practiced daily—even when her little strong-willed princess didn't want to practice. (We won't talk about those times.)

After the first few months of painful practice, something unexpected happened as I sat at my desk one day in school.

"Can anyone in the class play the piano?" asked my stern

fifth-grade teacher. Before I realized it and didn't know why she asked, my hand went straight up. I don't understand why I raised my hand. I had only been taking lessons for a short time—a very short time.

She looked at me and said, "Good," in her usual stern voice. "Come to the piano. I need you to play for our class to sing in the upcoming school Easter program."

"Will you need someone to turn the pages for you?" she asked. I hesitated and could not process her question.

With a piece of sheet music in one hand, the much-feared teacher rolled the other hand like a spinning wheel attached to her wrist, impatiently motioning for me to hurry forward; too late for me to back out now. If only I hadn't raised my hand. The situation was unfolding and certainly out of my control.

In a surreal fog, I approached the teacher and took the sheet music from the hand that wasn't spinning. When I read the title, "In Your Easter Bonnet," and then glanced at the music, it confirmed my worst fears—it was too advanced for me.

The teacher's face was now two shades darker red than the rouge she had applied to her high cheekbones earlier that day.

The teacher was emphatic about asking her original question again as she peered over her reading glasses perched on the end of her nose, "Will you need someone to turn the pages for you?" as if I had a hearing problem. I didn't have a hearing problem. It was a playing problem, but I was afraid to tell her.

I wanted to say, "Please ask someone else to play. I'll be glad to turn the pages." But my throat was so dry I couldn't speak. I just nodded.

I made a right turn toward the piano. I glanced over at the classroom exit door opening into the hallway. Seeing a

STORY 4: The Mask

possible escape route, I fought off a big impulse to run for the door. I managed to stay on the path to the piano bench, although the door option still looked pretty good.

By then, Larry, a boy who had nearly fallen out of his desk to volunteer as the page-turner, had beaten me to the piano. Several times, he had told me, "You're the prettiest girl in school." (Obviously, beauty is in the eye of the beholder.)

There he stood, smiling so proudly. How could I embarrass Larry, who seemed so pleased that I could play the piano?

As I settled onto the piano bench, my mother's words echoed: "Stomach in. Sternum high. Shoulders back." I focused on my posture, readying myself for the calamity ahead.

My trembling fingers touched the piano keys. Then, as if by some miraculous intervention, a newfound confidence surged through me, and my hands moved across the keyboard with a grace I had never known.

Divine enablement had come to my rescue. My fingers danced over the piano keys, and what I heard surprised me. It sounded just like "In Your Easter Bonnet!"

Little did I know that a similar thing would happen again after I became a married woman with two adult children. I was asked to be one of the speakers for a weekend retreat for ministry leaders. Though I felt woefully inadequate, God broke through again with divine help. I experienced the same confidence that had suddenly enveloped me at the piano many years earlier.

~~~

WEEKEND RETREAT FOR MINISTRY LEADERS

At a spotlight moment, have you ever wished you were someone else? Or even wondered if you should be there. Even worse, did you feel you weren't qualified to be a speaker and had no clue why you said "Yes" when asked to speak?

I have! The moment arrived, and it was my turn to speak at the retreat. I hadn't intended to be someone else, but I realized that is precisely what I did.

Later, I read about "imposter syndrome." I would have been a perfect case study. This phenomenon can occur in various ways, including work, academics, and personal relationships. It can lead to feelings of stress, anxiety, and self-doubt.

Barbara, my dear friend and mentor, spoke on the opening night. I've enjoyed working with her for many years in the Joysprings ministry. She's a gifted speaker, an excellent leader, and a teacher.

Barbara delivered an eloquent and inspiring message on the retreat's first night. Her deep connection with God was evident as she shared her message. It was punctuated with numerous scriptures and interwoven with scenes from her life story.

As Barbara spoke, I noticed everyone was deeply touched. Some scrambled to find a pen and paper to take notes. I was one of them. I wanted to remember every one of her golden nuggets.

Before I arrived, I studied intensely to prepare my talk for the second night. Nevertheless, after listening to Barbara, I decided my preparation wasn't good enough.

Have you ever felt that you just were not enough?

The following day, I excused myself from the free-time activities, locked myself in my room, and frantically worked to rewrite my notes. Like Barbara, I held my Bible and "updated" notes when I stood to speak that night. I never suspected what happened next!

When I began to speak, I only remembered my original notes and then took off like the storyteller I am. Every life story became funnier and funnier. The more the audience laughed, the more I laughed. The stories kept soaring like a

STORY 4: The Mask

rocket at takeoff. I even shared stories I had never shared publicly before. Something was in motion, and I was exhilarated!

I never thought to look at my new notes which I had passionately hugged the whole time, without realizing it. Even though I had exhausted myself working to revise my speaking notes earlier that day, I felt a rush of life as my energy rushed into supercharge mode.

I felt like a locomotive rolling down the tracks at full speed! I heard my life stories flowing out, empowered by the Lord, and stood amazed at what was happening. Joy coursed through my spiritual veins as I told about what a difference God made in my life. Some stories brought holy quietness and tears. Others sparked a roaring laughter.

Afterward, one lady with a lovely British accent exclaimed, "I laughed so hard I nearly fell off my stool. Oh, I needed to laugh!"

HOLY AWARENESS MOMENT
I had spent unnecessary hours comparing myself to my dear friend, then rewriting my talk to put on my "gifted Barbara" mask. However, the moment I began speaking, the "mask" fell off, and God replaced it with a warm hug from above, affirming His unique design for me.

As I observe others like Barbara who have found their place in God's kingdom, I rejoice in their beautiful discovery of their Jesus-shaped identity. I, too, have found my place in Him.

MORE...
By rightly attributing all glory to God and not seeking it for ourselves, we are transported to the highest limits of what He will accomplish through us.

It is a divine mystery how God deposits His Holy Spirit, His presence, within us when we become His followers. He teaches and guides us, showing us the pathway for our lives.

The glory of God shines through His creation, with nature echoing the majesty of its Creator. Within every person lies a beautiful "musical chord" of life placed by the same Creator. Allowing God to play this chord results in a divine sound that gives rhythm and meaning to life. ~

For we are God's handiwork, created in Christ Jesus to do good works, which God prepared in advance for us to do.
(Ephesians 2:10)

STORY 5

Bees and Roses

The Joy of the Ageless

The telephone's piercing ring beside my bed shattered the quiet of that early Sunday morning. It was Mother. "I don't think it will be long. Come as fast as you can."

My dad was dying. Hands trembling, I jumped out of bed, grabbed some clothes, and started getting dressed while trying to hang up the phone.

All I could think to pray was, "I've got to get there before... please, God, let me talk to my dad one more time." Even though he was a good person, he was a quiet man about his faith in God, and I wanted assurance that he was ready to go to Heaven.

Somehow, even though I was in a daze, I finished dressing. Memories accompanied me on the short but long twelve-mile trip to my parent's home.

Dad, a quiet, handsome man, had always been physically strong and passionate about all his interests. The successful construction business he and my Mother started early in their marriage, when their family was young, contributed to his physical strength.

His arms looked like the baking soda box picture of the muscular man's arm. Even into his seventies, he remained strong and healthy. Although the last few weeks had robbed him of strength, he still appeared strong. He had not been sick long enough to become frail. Standing beside Mother in the church vestibule only five weeks earlier, he had greeted people as they entered. We had no clue that he had colon cancer. Neither did he.

God did answer my prayer. When I arrived, Mother met me at the door of their home. I learned that Dad was, indeed, still alive. She walked with me to the room where he lay on a hospital bed. He was motionless, eyes closed. Mother stepped out to give us time alone, and I still cherish those priceless moments with Dad. I moved in close to him and wrapped his hand around my own. Believing he could hear me, I expressed my love and appreciation to him for being such a good dad. Then, I asked, "Dad, is your heart right with God?"

He appeared to be unconscious, but I asked anyway, "If your heart is right with God, squeeze my hand." Immediately, I felt his hand gently squeeze mine.

Our family gathered around his bed as the time lengthened between his breaths. I was touching one of Dad's muscular arms as his last earthly breath came—ushering in that shocking, final goodbye. Sad tears trickled down our cheeks as we helplessly stood by our family hero. His life journey was about to take him away from us—beyond the confines of Earth. What would it be like for him?

I couldn't believe what I did next. Something took over.

STORY 5: Bees and Roses

It was quick and instinctive. Give Dad a sendoff from Earth with music. Immediately, I heard myself burst into song. Mother joined in. "Jesus loves me; this I know."

Suddenly, an overwhelming sense of joy surged through me. It transported me from the heaviness of that moment to the realization that I knew what Dad was experiencing. You see, I had also made that heavenly journey.

MY JOURNEY: THE SURPRISE ANNOUNCEMENT

A few years before this, during my early morning time with God, I heard Him speak within my spirit. (I now recognized His voice quickly from past encounters.) I leaned into Him to hear Him make this incredible and exciting announcement.

"I will have a special blessing for you in Richmond," He said.

In two weeks, we would be traveling to Richmond, Virginia, to attend a teen talent competition. For several years, I'd been working with a teenage music ensemble. They were highly talented. They had just won the regional division of a church-sponsored teen talent competition, and their next destination was the national competition in Richmond, Virginia.

Thinking ahead, my mind was in high gear, trying to guess what kind of blessing God would shower me with. I also tried to picture where I would encounter it. Later, I realized that there was no earthly way I could have imagined the magnitude of the gift that awaited me. I would experience an encounter that forever changed my perspective on life, death, and me. I was so excited. I couldn't wait to tell Lavon, my husband, when he came home for lunch. I knew he would join in the anticipation of what was to unfold.

Later that same day, Barbara James, a close friend, called and asked if I would participate in an early morning prayer vigil she was organizing. Guess where it would be! It was in

Richmond at our annual church conference following the talent event.

"Yes!" I quickly replied. Barbara was one of my deeply spiritual friends, so I shared what I had heard from God that morning. She knew that a prayer room session was my cup of tea! I had learned to appreciate and listen to prayers from people who prayed much more profoundly than I did. I hoped to grow to be like them someday. They seemed to have a "dimension" I was missing in my relationship with God.

"Indeed," I told myself, "A prayer room is where I will encounter my special blessing!" Again, I was trying to predict God's surprise and even set the stage for Him. I thought I had it all figured out.

THE RED ROSES

The two weeks before the trip passed quickly. In Richmond, our teen instrumental ensemble did well. To add to my joy, my talented musicians surprised me with a dozen red roses to express their appreciation for my leadership.

The following day, the teenagers packed the church van to drive back to Athens. Lavon and I were packing our car to move from the Richmond Hyatt to the Marriott, where the early morning prayer sessions would be held—the location of my highly anticipated special blessing, I thought. But God had a different plan in mind.

As I carefully placed my beautiful bouquet of roses in the car, I suddenly felt a sharp pain on the top of my right shoulder. With a startled gasp, I jumped back and grabbed my shoulder. One of my friends, Joyce, rushed to my side and said, "I think you just got stung!" She exclaimed, "I saw a bee fly away from your shoulder."

STORY 5: Bees and Roses

THE CALL FOR HELP

I knew that sometimes the bee's stinger is left inside the wound. I assumed it would be a simple matter of removing it, but I needed help since I couldn't reach that area of my shoulder. I headed to our second-floor room, where I knew Laura, our daughter, was packing. By the time the elevator reached the second floor, I began to feel anxious.

As I stepped off the elevator, I saw Laura exit our room. "I've just been stung, I said frantically. "I need your help to remove the stinger from my shoulder."

Laura responded, "Oh no, I can't get back into the room. Dad has the key." She left immediately to find her dad.

When she reappeared with the key, I cried, "Please tell Dad I need him. I'm feeling very strange." Now shaken by the urgency in my voice, she quickly unlocked the door, escorted me into the room, and took off running to look for her dad again. When Lavon rushed into the room, I said, "I feel strange."

"You're just hyperventilating," he said in his usual calm, steady manner. "Lie down on the bed, and I will wet a cloth with cool water for your face."

While he was still running the water over the washcloth, I told him that my tongue felt thick. Not only that, but my face was beginning to feel numb. At that point, the calm exterior left Lavon's face. He quickly placed the cold cloth on my face and grabbed the telephone beside the bed.

I heard him shout, "Call for an ambulance. My wife has been stung." At this point, I thought *he* might be the one hyperventilating! I couldn't believe he had called for an ambulance. I had never heard of anyone dying from a bee sting.

Almost immediately, the phone rang. It was an EMT with specialized heart response training. Somehow, he was aware of the call for the ambulance. "I am in the area and will also stop by." We were assured that help was on the way. He arrived moments later, just before the ambulance.

THE STRETCHER ON WHEELS

My life was strangely out of control. Lavon leaned over me and prayed. Then, with his face no more than inches away from mine, he said, "Honey, the Lord is not through with you yet." I held onto those words as our two children, Laura and Christopher, stood beside my bed. I saw their lips silently moving.

Within minutes, I was surrounded by an emergency team. I didn't realize at the time that they were fighting to save my life. "If only they would just leave me alone and let me sleep," I thought. A stranger in a white uniform leaned over me and badgered me with questions. It felt like an intrusive barrage, but I now know that he was trying to keep me conscious. He told me they were about to do many procedures in quick succession.

Needles began piercing my swelling body, and oxygen tubes were placed in my nose. I heard the medic's communication with the hospital via a radio system, but it was muted, as if way off in the distance. His tone of voice sounded urgent as he relayed that I was not responding to the medication they had administered. The room became even busier, in a life-saving frenzy, when they realized they were losing me.

"We've got to get her to the hospital!" someone urgently yelled. A stretcher on wheels arrived beside my bed.

I was jolted to attention, and I'm pretty sure I looked mortified when I heard they were going to lift me off the bed and place me onto the stretcher. As out of it as I was, I still inwardly chastised myself, thinking, "Why didn't I stick to those weight-loss diets?"

When the paramedics leaned over to lift me from the bed, a rush of adrenaline came to my rescue. Feebly,

STORY 5: Bees and Roses

I announced, "I can do this myself." With my remaining strength, I lifted myself and sat on the side of the bed where the stretcher awaited me. Little did I know I was going to a place where my extra pounds didn't matter. I suppose neither life nor death nor anything in between can quell a woman's pride. Even if she's dying, she'll try to get up. I still didn't realize I was dying.

They helped me onto the stretcher and rushed me into the hallway. Lined up on each side of the hallway was a sad-faced group of teenagers and bystanders. I remember just wanting to sleep, unaware of my condition's seriousness.

I felt the stretcher bump against the side of the hotel elevator as it transported us to the ground floor, where the ambulance waited for me. The last thing I remember was looking up and seeing the bottom of the portable oxygen tank swinging over my head. Then, I lost consciousness.

Had I remained conscious, I am sure fear would have consumed me: Who would mother my two children? Will my husband remarry? I would have found comfort in the thought of our family rallying to help Lavon with the children. However, the idea of other women rallying around my husband would have been unsettling. Fortunately, I didn't have the chance to consider those delicate life issues.

THE AMBULANCE

Lavon told me what happened next. He said, "I jumped into the front passenger seat of the ambulance. I don't remember if I had permission to ride, but I wouldn't let it leave without me." Lavon continued, "Soon, one of the EMTs working on you in the back of the ambulance yelled to the driver, "Slow down! If we can't get her to respond, there's no need to rush to the hospital."

THE PASSAGEWAY
Since that life-changing day, I have struggled to express my experience with adequate words. Yet, the events of that day remain vivid and alive within me. My physical senses no longer existed. I learned quickly from first-hand experience that we are more than just a body. My soul and spirit survived physical death and entered a different realm of existence.

My journey took me into a round-shaped portal, a long passageway. It was softly lit by an overhead glow of light that seemed to have no source. It was just there. I sensed I had feet and legs but didn't have to use them to move. I traveled as if my body flew in an upright position. I moved swiftly toward a tall, wide, closed door at the end of the passageway. The door's upper half shone like polished metal, yet it looked as if it would have felt like leather if I touched it. The warm overhead light made the door visible.

Even outside the door, I felt snuggled by the intimacy in the atmosphere. Unrestricted freedom, majestic peace, wonder, and awe enveloped me. I felt secure, loved, and welcomed. I had stepped from Earth into the womb of eternity and knew I was headed to Heaven.

The closer I got to the door, the stronger I felt joy, celebration, and excitement radiating from the other side. I couldn't see beyond the threshold, but the door was now open just wide enough to step through. Then, before I could take that step, I stopped moving forward. An even more exciting surprise awaited me there.

HOLY AWARENESS MOMENT
I feel so limited when I try to describe the indescribable. I pray you have a Spirit-inspired imagination as you read this.

Suddenly, a holy presence filled the atmosphere. It was God! I knew it was Him, my God. I had been invited into His all-consuming holy presence. Joy danced within me. The

STORY 5: Bees and Roses

tenderness and love I felt are beyond description. I sensed His excitement that I was there.

They say a baby in the womb is comforted by the mother's heartbeat. Though the baby hasn't seen their mother yet, the baby recognizes her. Well, I recognized God. Although I didn't see His face, I knew it was Him. The atmosphere, filled with love and intimacy, was so palpable that I "felt" my head on His chest. I could feel and hear the "beat" of His heart.

The excitement I felt was so intense that I couldn't remain silent. My heart was bursting with joy. Spontaneously, these words passionately flowed from my heart, "Dispose of me according to the wisdom of Your pleasure. May Your will be done through my own undoing."

I did not remember my life on Earth through all these holy moments. Yet, I had spoken the words of a prayer by St. Augustine, which I had written in my journal years earlier, and prayed many times on Earth.

Being there was amazing! I could move without using my feet and legs, and my thoughts became spoken words. Though I had never experienced anything like this, I still felt like myself, just more alive—exceedingly more alive than ever before.

BACK ON EARTH

I was anxious to enter the open door, to see Him in His fullness, the One my heart already knew was there. As I lifted one "foot" to step across the threshold, I was suddenly transported back to an Earthly consciousness. I heard, "Get moving! Get moving! She's responding!

Lavon said one of the EMTs, still working on me in the back of the ambulance, yelled out those words to the driver. My eyelids were too heavy to open, but I was conscious of a flurry of motion around me. I knew when my stretcher was unloaded from the ambulance and was forcefully rolled across the threshold into the hospital. Once inside, I felt a needle pierce the top of my right hand. It was full of something that made my body tremble and shake.

Lavon told me later that as he stood nearby, a nurse placed her hand on his back and said, "Your wife is going to be all right." At that point, he started trembling, fighting back the tears.

The staff placed me in the Intensive Care Unit, where a nurse sat at the foot of my bed all night, closely monitoring my heart.

The next day, I asked for a telephone as soon as I could. I knew Mother needed to hear my voice. I can still hear her beautiful voice when she answered, "Hello."

When she realized it was me, Mother exclaimed, "Oh, darling!" and then gushed, "We've been so concerned! I've waited for your call. I was only comforted when God told me... 'I'm taking care of her.'"

THE INTERSECTION

On the third day, just before the hospital released me from ICU, a young man came to my room. He introduced himself as the EMT from the ambulance. "I just wanted to see you alive," he said. "You gave us a terrible scare." He paused, "We almost lost you."

I knew the exact moment he was referring to. I had been on a journey that led to the intersection of Earth and Heaven. I had seen the limits of everything human and had experienced the joy that awaits God's child. Now, I no longer just hope. I know.

WHAT YOU TAKE WITH YOU WHEN YOU DIE

"You can't take anything with you when you die" is often recited. But there is something we do take with us when the "silver cord" is broken and we enter the passageway beyond earthly existence: It is our personal relationship with God!

THE SPECIAL BLESSING
I never set foot in the prayer room at the Marriott in Richmond, where I had expected to receive what I thought would be my special blessing. I certainly never could have guessed that it would be wrapped with cords of death.

Yet, my heart beats and still expands with wonder and thankfulness when I think about just how special my blessing is, for I was granted a sacred glimpse into the divine realm of holy mystery. I basked in the presence of Almighty God.

At God's pleasure, He continued my mission on Earth, forever infused with a taste of Heaven! My husband was right. God was not through with me yet. Even now, my heart burns with the second chance I was given to tell others about our loving, perfect God!

BACK TO THE HOTEL ROOM
After I was released from the hospital, Lavon and I returned to the hotel room to rest for a couple of days before making the 8-hour drive back home. On the day of our departure, Lavon packed for us both and loaded the car.

Before walking out the door of our room, I turned and looked at the bed where I lay dying only days before. With a new confidence, I said, "Lord, I don't know why You spared my life, but I commit the rest of my time here to fulfilling Your plan for me."

On Earth, I remain imperfect, flaws and all, yet my awareness of belonging to the Kingdom of Heaven is heightened. A re-ignited passion fuels my desire to live out God's plan for me.

I feel like a champion bursting forth from the starting line. With my second chance, my heart beats with the words of Isaiah:

"For the Lord God will help me; therefore I will not be disgraced; therefore I have set my face like a flint, and I know I will not be ashamed (Isaiah 50:7)."

FROM THE MOUTH OF A BABE

After Dad moved from Earth, word spread throughout the rest of the house to waiting relatives and friends who had quietly respected our last moments with him. Holding our two-year-old granddaughter, Victoria, Lavon stepped into the room where we were still gathered around Dad's bedside.

Little Victoria looked across the room at her great-grandfather lying silently on the bed. Everyone was astonished and comforted when she announced, "He's happy now!"

She was too young to know about life and death and too young to see the significance of the moment, yet we understood the importance of the words she had spoken. Dad was in Heaven!

MORE …

There is another side. As a young girl, I often heard Ms. Mary, a lady who attended the same church I did, testify about her near-death experience.

"I was not a Christian when I died," she said. Then, she proceeded to describe a horrifying, hellish experience. She was grateful God allowed her to come back and warn others.

A Christian's death is merely a transformation from the lower life to the higher life. Those on Earth call it death, but the angels call it birth. Colossians 1:18 tells us that Christ is called the "firstborn from the dead."

This expression emphasizes Christ's resurrection and the unique position He holds as the one who conquered death

STORY 5: Bees and Roses

and paved the way for the resurrection of believers. Christ stands supreme above all and is holy forever! ~

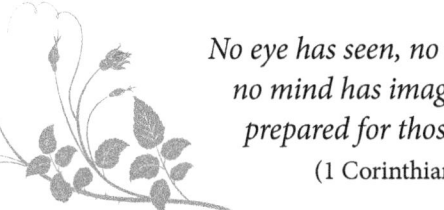

No eye has seen, no ear has heard, and no mind has imagined what God has prepared for those who love him.
(1 Corinthians 2:9 NLT)

STORY 6

The Fight to Breathe

The Joy of the Little Green Bag

The following story is written by our daughter, Laura Revells Allen. It tells of love, hope, empathy, and the unexpected.

It all began in January of 2020 when life was still normal, and the world was filled with excitement for what the new year had to offer. The year began much like the previous years, with fireworks, celebration, and prayer. I was an online ESL (English as a Second Language) teacher to young students in China.

I loved these precious little children and would pray for them. I prayed that they would feel and experience God's love, and I also prayed for their health and safety.

You see, China was under a mandatory quarantine in many provinces for this new virus called "COVID-19." Some of my sweet students had been unable to play outside with friends, or even leave their apartments for months. I had sympathy for them, but I could not empathize with them. I mean…it was a world away and wouldn't affect us, right? I met with some of these children several times a week. For some, it was their only outlet outside of their tiny apartments. As horrible as this new virus seemed, my students were safe. I was safe. My family was safe.

THE NEW PLAGUE

On January 18, 2020, everything changed! COVID-19 made its way to the USA. By this time, the US was panicking over this new virus! It was dreaded like the plague; in fact, it was the new plague. There has never been a communal illness in my lifetime that was so dreaded. It was so feared that it tempted to remove all humanity from one who was threatened by a "carrier." If someone looked like they might cough, they were treated like a leper. There were even recorded hair-pulling fistfights in stores where one person refused to wear a mask, invoking the anger of another.

I believe this virus was an attack from the pit of hell, and it was awful! However, this story is about the GREATNESS of God. I will tell you some of the details about my journey and how He was in every little detail!

THE LITTLE COUGH

One morning, July 8th, 2020, to be exact, while teaching a precious student named Peter, I had a strange little cough. My young student's face was concerned as he blurted, "Oh, teacher, you have the COVID." Outwardly, I assured him that I didn't. However, inwardly, my thoughts whimpered, could I?

As a family, my husband Greg, son Chase, and two daughters—Victoria and Olivia, and I had taken great precautions against this new virus. We had shut the door on the proverbial Ark and were safe inside. There was no way

STORY 6: The Fight to Breathe

I could have "the COVID," or could I?

That strange little cough quickly invited "friends." By the end of the day, I had developed a horrible headache and what felt like a bad sinus infection. The words of my young student would pop up in my mind's ears, but I quickly suppressed them. I replaced those words with thoughts that I just had a sinus infection. However, more "friends" were soon added to the trifecta of symptoms.

I began feeling extremely fatigued and started running a fever, which rose to 104 degrees. Then, the tell-tale sign presented itself. I decided to spray an aromatic disinfectant to kill any germs in the air and quickly realized my sense of smell was gone. I joked, "Why couldn't it have been my sense of taste? Maybe I could lose some weight during this ordeal. You know, maybe something good could come out of this." Well, as the adage goes, "Be careful what you wish for." The next day, my joke was not so funny. Everything I ate tasted like cardboard with a heaping seasoning of salt.

THE DREADED TEST RESULTS

I soon realized I had something more than a sinus infection. I took a COVID test, and it came back positive. My doctor said to stay home, and if my oxygen levels dropped below 90, I would need to go to the hospital. Although Greg tested positive for COVID two days after I had, his symptoms seemed to be very mild. This would later change.

My symptoms had progressed to a very serious stage by this point, and my husband was becoming progressively concerned.

Speaking of my husband, I knew from the first date that this man was going to be my husband. God connected our spirits before we even met, which is a different story for another time. Life can throw difficult things at couples and families. But as a couple, we resolved in our hearts and minds that, with God, we would weather these storms together in the same boat. It is sometimes in the midst of the most challenging times that we get to see the depth of our love for one another. I knew that Greg loved me, but it was during this life-threatening ordeal that our love and bond grew to new depths.

THE HOSPITAL

I continued to get worse, and on July 15, it was evident things were not going so well for me! I monitored my oxygen levels with a Pulse Oximeter and was no longer able to keep my oxygen up to 90. My lungs started crackling when I breathed. Our hospital did not have a very good reputation, so I told Greg that if I had to be hospitalized to please take me to Emory. But God was in those details, too.

During the night, Greg said I spoke out in my sleep and said, "It's not about the hospital; it's about the doctors." He said I was wheezing all through the night. The next morning, I could hardly breathe. My oxygen saturation level was now in the 80s, so Greg called the paramedics. We were told the paramedics would meet us outside our front door. They refused to come inside. So, I was sitting on a bench on the front porch, and Greg was standing on one of the steps to our porch when they arrived.

The paramedic did a quick check and told me I wasn't that sick. He said that the hospital would probably send me home. I told the paramedic that I wanted to go to Emory. He kept telling me I wasn't that sick, and my lungs sounded clear. Even though I felt horrible, I started questioning myself, wondering if I was overreacting, so I said, "Well, I guess I won't go." After all, I was terrified about going to the hospital. It was still in the early stages of the initial strain of COVID-19 in the US. Fear-inducing information was circulating on social media, but much was still unknown. Many people

STORY 6: The Fight to Breathe

feared that if they went to the hospital with COVID-19, they would not make it out alive. I guess a part of me tried to convince myself that the paramedic was correct, even though my body was screaming he was wrong.

ANOTHER EMERGENCY

About that time, I looked, and Greg had this strange stare as he started leaning forward. He was passing out. I feared he would hit his head on the concrete steps, so I yelled, "Catch him!" The paramedic caught Greg's head in his hands an instant before his head hit the step, a miracle within itself. The paramedic quickly changed his tune and said, "Your husband is the emergency now, and you're going, too!"

Now, the decision of which hospital we would be taken to was in the hands of the paramedic. From the look of panic on his face, I knew it would be the closest one.

The paramedic called a second ambulance to transport each of us separately to the hospital. Imagine the scene in front of our house: There were two large fire trucks (which they always send for some reason) and two ambulances. There we were, sitting on our front porch, waiting to be loaded into our chariots and whisked off to the hospital. I can only imagine what our neighbors were thinking as they saw two gurneys being rolled across our lawn early that morning. Looking back, I can see so much humor in that scene.

They took us to the nearest hospital, the one I DIDN'T want to go to. But I didn't care at that point. I was immediately admitted, but to my surprise they sent Greg home that night.

JUST IN TIME

The doctors said I was severely ill and had double pneumonia. I was so sick that I probably wouldn't have made it had I stayed home. It was the beginning of a 12-day stay in the hospital. My viral load was rapidly increasing.

The words I spoke to Greg, "It's not about the hospital, but it's about the doctors," were true. The doctors were very concerned and worked hard to help me. If Greg had not passed out, I would have gone somewhere else or would have possibly died at home. I was in the right place with the right doctors. God was in the details.

THE LITTLE GREEN BAG

After I was wheeled to my private room, a sweet nurse started setting everything up for my stay. The door to the room was open, and I got a glimpse of a cart full of colorful gift bags, which quickly rolled past my door. The nurse also happened to see the cart as it passed by. She said, "I will get you one." I wasn't really sure what they were, but I said, "Okay."

The nurse left the room briefly and returned with a pretty little lime-green gift bag decorated with colorful stickers. I was too ill to even care to look inside the bag, so the nurse set it on my cart, which also doubled as a bed tray. I actually wouldn't look inside the bag until the day I was discharged, but just seeing it sitting there throughout my 12-day stay brought me joy.

I wasn't sure why it brought me joy. Maybe it was the color of the bright and cheerful lime green bag and stickers, or perhaps it was that someone or a group of people poured their hearts into making these bags for COVID-19 patients. Could it have been the love I felt from their gesture?

I now think it was all of the above. It didn't matter what was in the bag; it was just the fact there was a bag lovingly made by strangers for people like me. It brought me hope, comfort, and a sense of peace. I received beautiful flowers after I was admitted. As my situation continued to decline, the doctors decided to move me to ICU. The flowers were not allowed to go with me, but they allowed the little green bag to accompany me on my journey.

STORY 6: The Fight to Breathe

Despite everything going on, I felt at peace! No one was allowed to visit or stay with me in the hospital, but I never felt alone. I knew God was with me. I knew many people were praying for me because I could feel their prayers. I knew that strangers had shown love to someone they had never met by putting together the contents of the little green bag.

Again, God was in the details.

A GOOD GOD

How good is our God that He can comfort us and show His love through complete strangers? How powerful is the spiritual bond that knits God's children together? Knowing that, no matter what transpired, I knew in my spirit that all was well.

This peace was reflected in the way I answered people's questions. When the doctor asked me how I was doing, I said, "I am doing well and can probably go home soon." However, in the natural, I was rapidly declining according to medical tests and observations. My body was headed for a complete shutdown. My lungs could not keep up with the needed oxygen, and I was in metabolic stress. Little did I know they were preparing to move me to the Intensive Care Unit.

SEVERELY ILL BUT NOT AFRAID

Although the doctors said I was extremely ill, I was never afraid. I knew God was with me. The Bible says, "God has not given us a spirit of fear but of power, love, and a sound mind (2 Timothy 1:7)." I was not afraid to die if that was God's time for me, but I believed that He was going to heal me. The doctors would come on any given day to ask how I was doing. I would continue to answer, "I'm doing great. Maybe I can go home in a day or two."

One doctor responded, "Well, you just keep being positive. We'll see how you are maybe next week." I thought it was such an odd thing for him to say. I had so much faith that God was going to heal me, and I could feel His presence with me so strongly that I thought I was getting better when I was actually getting worse. My spirit was speaking louder than my flesh, my body.

MY COMFORT

On July 21, they moved me to ICU. It was getting increasingly more difficult to keep my oxygen level up. It would drop to the 70s without supplemental oxygen. One night, a nurse told me they had me on the highest level they could give me and that if I could not keep my level at 90 or above with the forced oxygen, they would have to put me on the ventilator.

But God was with me. I sat up all night watching the monitor, praying, and breathing as hard as I could to keep from being put on the ventilator. I had heard it indicated a slim chance of survival.

I made it through the night with my oxygen just high enough so that I did not have to be put on the ventilator. However, I didn't seem to be getting better due to my high viral load. The inflammation continued to increase.

I was so sick that it was difficult to formulate the words to pray. This concerned me, but I knew that many people were holding me up in prayer. I thought back to one of my favorite Bible stories.

The children of Israel were fighting a battle. As long as Moses raised his arms, the Israelites were winning the battle. After a while, Moses' arms grew tired, so Aaron and Hur held his arms up for him. All the prayers going up for me were imparting the strength I needed to hold up my arms. The prayer warriors were helping me win the battle—the battle for my life.

STORY 6: The Fight to Breathe

HOLY AWARENESS MOMENT
In those darkest of hours, God ministered to me personally through a dream that He had given me many years earlier. I dreamt that I was alone in a room. It was bright, the walls were extremely tall, and there was no ceiling. I was kneeling on the floor, and Satan was hovering above me, laughing and taunting me. I felt so defeated. I cried out to God to help me. Then, I looked up and saw The Lord's hand. He said, "Just say, 'In the Name of Jesus.'" So, I did. And, as I said, "In the name of Jesus" over and over, Satan started falling, and I started rising.

The plotline turned dramatically. Satan was the one cowering on the floor, and I had been given victory! God reminded me through the dream that the name of Jesus is more powerful than anything the enemy can use to come against us. So, that night in the hospital, I just said, "Jesus" over and over again.

"The tongue has the power of life and death, and those who love it will eat its fruit (Proverbs 18:21)."

WARFARE
There was a moment when I had just had enough! I was filled with Holy anger. I entered into spiritual warfare, and I warred!

I had these weapons of truth, and I knew how to use them. I had been trained since I was young on how to use my spiritual "sword," the Bible. I believe the Holy Spirit gave me revelation about this "novel" COVID-19. COVID is the Latin word for crown. I believe it got this name because the spike proteins surrounding the virus cell resemble a crown. I saw this virus as a mocking spirit that dared to wear a "crown."

DAVID AND GOLIATH
The story of David and Goliath came to mind. The reason

David got so angry at Goliath was because he heard the giant mocking the God of Israel. So, David picked up three stones and defeated the giant, Goliath. I, too, got angry thinking about this mocking spirit trying to take authority over my body.

I picked up my first stone of warfare—worship (Psalm 149:6). I praised Jesus as the King of kings and Lord of lords.

I picked up my next stone of warfare (Ephesians 6:10-18), and I prayed that any open "door" that allowed the virus into my body would be closed.

I then picked up my third stone of warfare (Luke 9:1-2). I made a declaration that there is only One who has the authority to wear the crown in my life, and that is Jesus Christ. He is the King of kings! He paid the price at Calvary for my salvation and shed His precious blood for my healing. I then commanded the virus to leave my body in the name of Jesus Christ. I continued to worship and pray through the night and into the morning.

MESSAGE OF ENCOURAGEMENT
That very day, July 25, Mom sent me a message that a dear lady, Judy Ball, had just sent her. "By tomorrow, Laura will breathe with the Holy Spirit. His pure air. His life's blessings." God was in those details, too! He heard my prayer. God has equipped us to war in the spirit.

Up until that point, I had been declining rapidly. But *now*, there was a turnaround. My healing had begun! Sure enough, as Judy had said, the next day, the nurses came in and said I was beginning to improve. They were preparing for me to move to a regular room. On July 26, I was moved out of ICU!

DEFEATED ENEMY
When the enemy knows he has been defeated in one area,

STORY 6: The Fight to Breathe

he will try to attack through another door. That morning, Greg texted me that he had coughed up blood during the night. I encouraged him to get to the hospital immediately. They ran tests on him and found double pneumonia and blood clots in his lungs. He had a pulmonary embolism, and he was in tremendous pain! The warring began again, but this time, it was over the life of my dear husband. Although he was still in tremendous pain, he was treated with blood thinners and released from the hospital the next morning. Greg could have died from blood clots entering his lungs, but God intervened.

HOME
I was released to go home on July 28. When the doctor came in to talk to me, He said, "You were severely ill. You were talking out of your head." I'm not sure if he was referring to the times when I thought I was getting better when, actually, I was getting worse. Or, if they heard me passionately praying during the night. It was true that I was very ill, but I was never talking out of my head. I was "talking" from out of my spirit and faith.

After 12 days in the hospital and experiencing a miraculous healing, I was discharged. The doctor from the infectious disease area of the hospital came to my room before I left. She told me she just had to see me in person. She, and others, didn't think I was going to make it.

Although I still had a long recovery to complete healing, I was going home. To celebrate, I finally looked inside my beautiful lime green bag with the stickers on it. There was a note from a local church, a bottle of water, a notepad, and a pen. It is surprising how something so small can have such a big impact. It truly meant the world to me. I called the church that had put the bags together to thank them. The assistant pastor, who answered the phone, said that a group of ladies in the congregation had made the bags and had prayed over each of them. No wonder the little green bag with stickers brought me peace and joy.

NEVER AWAY FROM GOD'S LOVE

I would have never chosen to have gone through this experience with COVID-19, but the experiences I had with God, I would never trade. His goodness, His mercy, His love; all precious. His revelation of Himself; beautiful. The faith-building training; infinitely priceless. It overshadowed the difficult times I suffered.

Many people lost their lives to this horrible virus, a few we knew personally. My heart goes out to their families. I don't know why God chose to spare our lives, but I am thankful, and I don't take for granted that I get to spend more time with my beautiful family.

MORE ...

If you are alive today, it doesn't matter how old or young you are; God has a purpose for you here on Earth. Our loved ones who have gone to Heaven before us also had a purpose on Earth, and I believe they are still busy in Heaven. They didn't quit living just because they moved there. God said He would never leave us nor forsake us. He never left me. He was always with me throughout this entire journey, even in the smallest of details. ~

You saw me before I was born.
Every day of my life was recorded in Your
book. Every moment was laid out before a
single day had passed.
(Psalm 139:16 NLT)

STORY 7

Onward to the Nursery

The Joy Gift

Influencers hold great power. Proverbs 18:21 reminded us long before social media "that the tongue holds immense power over life and death." In fact, we all have the ability to influence others with our own stories that reflect God's power when we know Him.

Sharing our holy awareness moments with God impacts others for eternity. Personal stories inspire and uplift when we give God access to the hearts of those who listen.

Sometimes, God speaks to us in unexpected and profound ways. I encountered Him one night at our church's Women's Ministries Event. Sue, a lovely, petite Southern lady with beautiful blond hair, was the speaker. Her passion for God came through in her everyday life, even in the details.

That night, Sue shared the inspiring story of her "Joy Gift." It deeply impacted me. I am hopeful and prayerful that it will do the same for you.

Sue captured our attention with her first words: "I have learned firsthand, as Dr. Luke declares in Luke 1:37, 'that nothing is ever impossible with God.' Every single word comes with His power and the hope of fulfillment."

Her story, "Joy Gift," unfolded when Sue shared that in the fourteen and a half years leading up to 1979, she and her husband had struggled to conceive a child. After undergoing tests, their compassionate doctor informed them that they were unlikely to ever have children. Their devastation did not begin to fully describe their sorrow.

Devout Christians for years, Sue and her husband believed in the power of prayer. After the news that they might remain childless, Sue felt a strong urge to read through the Bible again. She woke up early every morning to make Bible reading a daily discipline.

Sue confided in her friend to pray for her. During the prayer, the friend received a compelling message from the Holy Spirit: "Your joy will come in 1979." Sue felt encouraged. Her heart danced at the announcement, and her friend's divine, prophetic prayer rested in her heart.

HOLY AWARENESS MOMENT

In March 1979, friends invited Sue and her husband to visit them in Tulsa, OK. While there, they invited them to attend a multi-night prayer event at a local university. They jumped at it and joined their friends for this unexpected privilege.

On the last night of the prayer event, after a great sermon on prayer, an invitation was given for those who wanted to receive prayer to come forward. Sue and her husband were deeply moved and decided to walk toward those in ministry, offering personal prayer.

Sue said, "The prayers prayed over us were spoken in such a way that I was confident that I would, indeed, have a

STORY 7: Onward to the Nursery

baby in 1979." When they returned to their seats, Sue looked over at her husband and, with a big smile, gave him the good news: "We're going to have a baby!"

They had no idea how God would answer their prayers. Would they conceive a child, or would their joy come through adoption? However, they had no doubt. This was the year!

During their next visit, their doctor mentioned that he had occasionally worked with birth mothers who chose to give their baby life—birth mothers who knew their baby was for someone else to raise, a person or couple dedicated to beautifully raising their child.

PREPARATION

Back home, while Sue was standing at her kitchen sink, she suddenly felt the strong impression to prepare the nursery. Not knowing if they would have a boy or a girl, Sue chose a butterfly-printed wallpaper in various colors, including blue and pink. Shopping for baby furniture, she felt like she was floating on air. She admitted that it felt surreal when she purchased baby announcements to celebrate the arrival of their little one. Sue slipped into the nursery often, always singing songs of praise.

INTERESTING EVENT

Time seemed to drag, and waiting became difficult. Sometimes, she avoided the empty nursery, wondering if the prayer promise had slipped away. The expectant parents decided to fast and pray for their baby for three days. One morning, only days after they completed their fast, they opened their front door and found that a mother dog had delivered her pups on their doorstep! The incredible timing seemed like a sign from God.

THE TELEPHONE CALL

On December 11, 1979, the telephone rang at 9:00 am. When Sue answered, she heard their kind doctor's voice. She drew in her breath and froze. Could this be it? He said, "A baby girl was born. She is in the hospital nursery. I will meet you at the hospital to introduce her to you. What is the soonest you can get there?"

Sue and her husband grabbed their coats as soon as possible, rushed to the door, and drove as fast as possible. Parking and jumping out of their car, they ran into the hospital, where the doctor escorted them to a private lounge and went to get the baby from the nursery. The couple already knew this was the little one God had promised them!

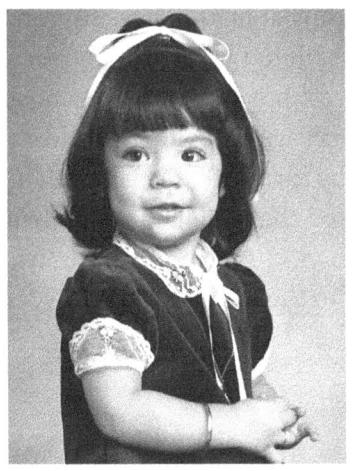

As the doctor walked in, he held the baby on his shoulder. They could only see the back of the baby's head, covered with thick, black hair. The excited couple immediately fell in love with her before even seeing her beautiful face!

"Two days later," Sue said, "We walked out of the hospital and took our precious, healthy baby girl home." Finally, their nursery with the butterfly wallpaper would have a sweet occupant.

JOY GIFT

"Our 'Joy Gift' did come in 1979," Sue exclaimed. "She arrived three weeks early, as she was not due until January of 1980. Her arrival was absolutely one of the happiest days of our marriage. We recognized that she was a sovereign miracle from God!"

STORY 7: Onward to the Nursery

God blessed the couple, too, in the details. Sue excitedly added, "Our baby was born exactly nine months after we were anointed at the prayer event in Tulsa."

What an incredible Christmas for their family of three, celebrating not only God's promise to them but the promise of God's only Son born in a manger.

MORE ...

The most important influence in our lives is reading and meditating on the Word of God, His "love letter" to us. When Sue shared in her testimony at the Women's Ministries Event that she was waking up early to read the Bible, I felt a tug in my heart. Her story compelled me to start each day before the break of dawn to read God's love letters.

At the time, I was in burnout mode. I was a "busy" Christian, involved in everything I thought I should be doing and everything I thought others expected of me as a leader. I felt liberated the morning God gently spoke to me, "I don't need you to work for me. I want to work through you." ~

Let the morning bring me word of your unfailing love, for I have put my trust in You. Show me the way I should go, for to You I entrust my life
(Psalm 143:8).

For no word from God will ever fail.
(Luke 1:37)

STORY 8

Get up! Throw Out the Line
The Joy of Redeemed Time

Andrew, a bright and cheerful eleven-year-old boy, lives with his family on a small farm known as Homesteader's Dream. One day, after finishing his meal, Andrew asked his father's permission to feed the food scraps to the chickens. Even though he had done this many times before, things did not turn out well this time.

After placing the food scraps in the container along the fence, Andrew went inside the fence line to check the chicken coop for fresh eggs. But, as Leader, the "ruling" rooster, saw the hens follow Andrew down to the lower coop, he charged Andrew and dug his spurs into each side of one of Andrew's knees, causing excruciating pain. Andrew tripped on a stump and rolled down a slight incline in his desperate escape before landing on his back.

Andrew lay still on the ground, his heart pounding

with fear as he tried to catch his breath. He dared not move a muscle, for he knew the rooster was still lurking nearby, waiting to unleash another vicious attack.

Meanwhile, Andrew's father grew increasingly worried when he realized his son had been gone too long. He called out Andrew's name, but all he heard in response was a high-pitched wail that sent shivers down his spine. Without hesitation, he rushed to his son's aid and, after seeing the extent of the injuries, scooped him up and carried him back to the house. There, the family gathered around him, tending to his wounds and trying to calm him down. Once Andrew regained his composure, his father took the opportunity to offer some advice: "Andrew, you can't let that rooster boss you around like that. It's time to show him who's in charge!"

~~~

Life is like that, isn't it? We can grow passive like Andrew when too many things are stacked against us. We are pinned to the ground, intimidated, and stuck in inertia. But God leads us to listen to Him for what's next. He will call us to rise from the ashes, face the roosters, and put feet to our faith.

A NEW BUSINESS
One morning, during my prayer time on our bedroom floor with my Bible open, I asked God to give me insight and direction about our financial needs. I was reading the book of Matthew. To pay their Temple tax, Jesus instructed His disciples: "But so that we may not cause offense, go to the lake and throw out your line. Take the first fish you catch; open his mouth, and you will find a four-drachma coin. Take it and give it to them for my tax and yours (Matthew 17:27)."

Getting up from the floor, I felt inspired to start a business; this verse became my blueprint. However, my lack of self-confidence whispered, "Are you sure you can do this? As a business owner, you would be in charge! But, in charge of what? Are you really serious about this?" But when God gives direction, He makes it clear.

Afterward, those who knew my natural giftings suggested starting a desktop publishing business. However, I was clueless about computers. Proficient in typewriting, yes, but I couldn't see how that would translate to working with a computer.

A helpful friend, who had recently graduated with a business degree and gone on to start his own business, advised me to enroll in a how to start a new business course offered by the Small Business Development Center at the University of Georgia.

Soon after, my new business was born: Great Works Creation Co., *Specialists in Visual Communications*! It was perfect. God knew how He had wired me. I have been creative since birth.

My business owner friend gave helpful additional advice. He encouraged me to be bold and confident when talking to potential customers, saying, "Yes, I can help you." He added that this approach helped him quickly understand what was needed to meet the customer's requirements.

HARDWARE OR SOFTWARE?

Soon, an unexpected opportunity arose for me to purchase a desktop publishing computer system. A friend, who sold computers, offered to help me unpack it. When I saw the new computer components being assembled, I realized how symbolic it all was of the new season I was in. God was in charge, and I was witnessing all the pieces coming together.

As we tackled the unopened boxes together, I thought of the first person I could call to "throw out my first line."

So, several days later, I took a deep breath, and with confidence born of the Spirit, called a potential client, managed to secure an appointment to discuss a plan, and with confidence born from blessing and obedience, I walked out the door with my first client, my first "catch."

On my way back from the appointment, I wondered, *What's the difference between hardware and software?*

Over twenty-five years later, Great Works Creation Co. is still in the business of designing visual communications. There have been a few first-place design recognitions. New doors of opportunity and connections continue to open!

~~~

Simultaneously, while journeying down the business road, God also developed my story-telling skills, and opened unexpected doors of opportunity.

LEGACY LEADERS EVENT

I drove to Atlanta to attend the annual Legacy Leaders event in a light rain. I wanted to get there before the predicted stormy weather arrived. I had been a group member for several years, contributing to their efforts through music and through designing and publishing marketing materials. That year, they asked me to be one of the speakers. My presentations always involved storytelling.

When I arrived outside of the hotel, nasty thunderstorms and dangerous weather were about to hit. I sat in my car, waiting for a hotel porter to help with my luggage.

Suddenly, the brightest shard of lightning exploded over my car, followed by the loudest clap of thunder I had ever heard. Torrential rain began to slap my car and everything in sight.

Due to the weather, the porter was slow to arrive, and I dared not get out of my car. Instead, I waited for the rain to subside. The storm lasted a while, enough time for me to settle with my thoughts.

I considered the defining events of my life and the accumulation of my God assignments. I had felt for a long time that not all of them had been fulfilled. I began to talk to God about it. "Is it too late for me? Have I missed the earthly assignments You planned for me?"

THE GREETING
When the rain stopped, a porter escorted me into the hotel, where a group of friends from Legacy Leaders welcomed me. One teased, "We knew that Arlette had arrived when we saw the flash of lightning and heard the loud thunder!" We all laughed together.

Little did I know what awaited me during the meeting.

HOLY AWARENESS MOMENT
After I spoke, a lovely lady asked if she could pray for me. I knew I was about to hear something extraordinary, so I got permission to record her prayer on my phone.

She said, "I enjoyed your testimony today about commitment and loyalty to the Lord. It was rich and powerful, and I thank God for your sacrifice. I especially appreciated how you encouraged us to trust the Lord about things we really don't understand yet."

"As you know," She continued, "God is good. He is the provider. He is the way maker. But the Lord says that He has called you and given you powerful and life-giving stories. You will eventually write them down, and they will jump off the page because they will pulsate with truth. Readers will know they are not fabricated, giving false hope of things that never materialize."

Her prayer continued. "The Lord says that He has given you a powerful testimony of *who He is*, and as you write what He shows you, your stories will flow out to others as rivers of living water. They will impart life and strength, showcasing divine order. The Lord says that He will be with you in a more palpable way. His anointing will rest on you, causing you to arise and go out, touched by glory."

I was stunned and so very humbled as she continued to pray. I had told no one about the question I had asked God earlier in my car. As she continued, she said, "The Lord says that you're late in discovering His purpose for you, but He's going to make up for lost time. You are like a slow-blooming flower, but the Lord will redeem the years and make up for any misplaced opportunities. Furthermore, you will not miss one connection in the future or ever run behind again. The Lord says He has kindled your fire and is causing you to burn brightly. As you return home this time, you will possess a passion and a zeal to work joyfully for the Kingdom of God."

I returned home, inspired and energized because God answered my question, "Is it too late for me?"

BACK HOME
Two days after returning home, I received a call asking if I would be available on short notice to be interviewed as an inspirational speaker on a television program in Atlanta.

With my new confidence, I responded, "Yes, I will." I was told that another guest on the same program would be interviewed: An ambassador from Israel.

Two weeks later, Lavon and I walked into the TV station. Introductions to the ambassador and her associate followed. We exchanged greetings with smiles. An observant bodyguard accompanied them.

The ambassador and her associate were interviewed first on the program. My interview followed. While I was on the air, the ambassador's associate found Lavon in the audience and invited us to attend a gala in Atlanta. She told Lavon, "A formal invitation will follow."

I came home in a daze, my fuses blown. I couldn't believe what was unfolding. Of course, my first thought was, "What should I wear to the gala?"

STORY 8: Get up! Throw Out the Line

The night of the ambassador's gala arrived. Lavon and I arrived early, so we stopped at a nearby coffee shop. This gave us time to quiet ourselves and talk to the Lord. Our prayer was simple: "Lord, we know You have opened this door. We ask that we don't miss any connections You have for us tonight."

At the gala's entrance, the ambassador, and her husband greeted us as we entered. She commented on the lovely jacket I was wearing.

The gala was in a large ballroom with many round, beautifully decorated tables. Opulent bouquets on top of the white linen tablecloths adorned the center of each one. Before we were seated, guests continued to mingle and introduce themselves to one another.

A charming couple introduced themselves to us: Arlene and Paul. After a short getting-to-know-one-another conversation, Paul suggested, "Let's exchange cards because we don't want this connection to fall through the cracks." When he said "connection," it echoed like a sweet song. Thus, our incredible friendship began.

A few weeks later, Arlene introduced us to a friend, Ellen, who was passionate about using the arts to inspire courage and ideals. This led to us being invited to join the executive board of Violins of Hope South Carolina. Our Violins of Hope events drew upwards of 10,000 South Carolinians in varying audiences, and in one month of concerts, in four major cities.

It was an adventure of joy to be involved in the planning and designing of the marketing materials for these concerts. When I was asked to join the board, I knew that it was something I couldn't turn down because music has always been a significant part of my life.

I can still remember the feeling of excitement I had when I began taking piano lessons in elementary school. My teacher introduced me to classical music, which opened up a whole new world. In high school, I had the opportunity to join the Glee Club, where I discovered the joy of singing with others. I continued singing as part of the college Singers and found that my love for music only grew stronger. Over the years, participating in church music has given me a sense of community and belonging that I've grown to cherish. Being able to share my passion for music with others has been an incredible gift.

ANOTHER INVITATION
As the ambassador drew near to retirement, she reached out to Lavon and me with another invitation, to attend a celebration event at The Temple in Atlanta.

I'll never forget that evening. As Lavon and I drove into the entrance of The Temple parking lot, one of many security guards motioned for us to stop. As he walked toward our car, I lowered my window. He recognized us from the TV interview and said, "I know you. Go on in!"

MORE ...
As wonderful as it felt to be recognized by the guard and given entrance to the temple, it pales in comparison to what God will say when He sees us approaching one day. Even now, He knows us intimately. On that day, He will invite us into His Kingdom without the slightest reservation, "I know you, come on in!" ~

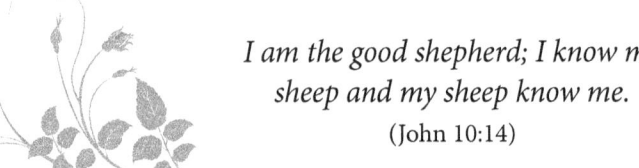

I am the good shepherd; I know my sheep and my sheep know me.
(John 10:14)

STORY 9

Stomach in, Sternum high, and Shoulders back

*Joy in the Face of Fear:
Passing the Baton of Confidence*

In this broken world, there's a lot that strikes fear in the hearts of mankind. Each of us has our own unique set of fears. I wish you and I could have some private time together because I would love to hear your stories. Fear can attack us in many unexpected ways. Sometimes, it seems like it's stalking us.

One day, I had a face-to-face encounter with a copperhead in our garage. When I got out of my car, I noticed movement near my feet. There he was, a 48-inch snake, coiled up tight, already in attack mode, making warning lunges that came within an inch of my bare legs.

In a desperate attempt to escape, I tried to get back in my car. I hit the back of my head hard on the doorframe. As I slammed the door shut, I looked around to see if the snake had come in with me. Isn't this the stuff of nightmares!

My husband heard my screams and ran into the garage to rescue me from whatever was causing me to cry out in terror. And at that moment, he was so focused on me that he didn't look down. Thankfully, he stepped right over the snake. The reptile, however, had already turned and was slithering away from the car. Lavon only saw the tail.

Although I was safely in the car, I couldn't stop screaming. Lavon opened the door and shouted, "HONEY, you've GOT to get hold of yourself!"

He had quite a time helping me out of the car because my knees were still buckled from fear. When we got inside, he saw my head injury, noted the swelling, and immediately took me to the nearest medical facility. The doctor assured us I would be okay. Then he said, "You do have a concussion, so don't be surprised if your head is sore in the morning.

The morning came, and I was terribly sore, alright, but it wasn't my head that was sore—it was my lungs!

DIFFERENT KINDS OF FEAR
Fear has so many faces. Sudden terrors can overtake us, the kind of terror I felt when I stumbled upon the copperhead, but it was only momentary. Other fears come on us slowly as we are forced to digest unexpected bad news. In one way, the latter is more traumatic. The snake incident was over in several minutes, but bad news can change the future. In the story I'll share next, the threat was not a snake bite. It was the life of my mother.

AN EVEN GREATER FEAR EVENT
A faint, sterile smell permeated the almost chilly room. The

STORY 9: Stomach in, Sternum high...

ceiling lights were dim, but one bright light was focused on the patient. It could have been a lone spotlight on a stage, a scene acted out in a play. All the characters stood by: a tall, young, well-dressed doctor with black hair; a very professional-looking nurse, wearing a wrinkle-free white uniform, holding a stainless-steel tool in her hand; and the patient who was about to hear the most shocking news of her life—my mother.

There I was, the family representative taking the one spot left in the room. Oh, how I wished it was just a church play like the many I had seen Mother act in. But this was not pretend. It was the real thing.

I nervously wrung my hands together, waiting for the doctor to speak. "Please, Lord," I prayed. "Please let the diagnosis be good!" After a few moments of looking into Mother's eye, the handsome specialist finally spoke, "You have an ocular melanoma growing inside your left eye." Realizing I should probably be taking notes, I scrambled in my purse for a piece of paper, but all I could find was a deposit slip. No blank paper of any kind was available. Probably just as well. I was feeling strange, feeling the edges of shock, and finding it hard to concentrate.

On the one hand, I should not have been so surprised. Mother's ophthalmologist discovered the tumor two days earlier during a routine eye exam. He had referred her to this retinal specialist. For two days our family and friends had been praying fervently.

Now, as I sat in the examination room, purse on my lap, feeling surreal, my heart screamed, "God, where are you? Didn't you hear our prayers?"

Mother, a beautiful woman, looked at the doctor and, ever so calmly, asked, "What are my options?"

The doctor explained in medical language. "Fifty years ago, enucleation was the only alternative."

"What's enucleation?" Mother asked.

The doctor answered, "Enucleation is the removal of the eye. But there is a relatively new type of treatment; radiation."

Mother remained calm despite the shock of the first option. I was amazed. Softly, she asked, "Which is the best?"

"We don't know, he explained. "That's the purpose of a study you can participate in if you so choose. The study is to determine the advantages and disadvantages of both procedures.

So, Mother had two options: Choose either procedure or become a participant in the study program. If she decided to participate in the program, one of the two procedures would be randomly assigned by a computer: 1.) Removal of her eye, or 2.) Radiation.

"I'll probably choose radiation," Mother said thoughtfully. "At least I would be able to keep my eye. Wouldn't that be better?"

The doctor looked at Mother with admiration. It was obvious he was surprised and impressed by how well she was taking the news. He assured her, "You don't need to decide right now. Go home, think about it, and we'll set up appointments for further evaluation to determine if the cancer is in any other part of your body."

I looked over at my mother sitting across the room in the examination chair, so prim and proper. 'Stomach in, sternum high, shoulders back,' just as she had instructed me many times growing up. Even though I was a married woman with two children, I suddenly felt like a little girl again. She was so composed, so mature, and I was aware of my fragility. Oh, this can't be happening to Mother!

BACK TO THE MOMENT

A loud metal clang jarred me back to the moment when the doctor accidentally dropped an instrument on the tray. It rattled whatever composure I had left. I wanted to scream, "God, how could You let this happen!"

The doctor then turned to me and asked, "Do you have any questions?" I slowly shook my head. I was just done in at that point and had trouble thinking. I wanted all of this to be over. If I could have found a door to exit the crisis itself, I would have grabbed Mother's hand, and we would have run for it!

OTHER TEST RESULTS
Trips back and forth to the Retinal Specialist's office, seventy-five miles away, occupied the next few weeks. "The news is good," the specialist said, looking up from the test results. "You don't have any other kind of cancer in your body, only the melanoma in your left eye. Have you decided which procedure you want?"

Mother looked down and shook her head, obviously still unsure. She asked, "How soon do you need to know? If possible, I want to attend my grandson's wedding in a few weeks." She was so relieved when the doctor assured her she could wait until after the wedding to announce her decision.

Mother began to lose weight during the next two weeks, and I knew exactly why. I grew up seeing her faith in action. She fasted and prayed, asking God for direction. Her leaner frame reminded me that she was living everything she had taught her children.

HOLY AWARENESS MOMENT
My phone rang early the morning after the wedding. It was Mother with an unshakable confidence in her voice. "Call the doctor. I want the first available appointment. I've made my decision."

She went on to explain, "In the middle of the night, a bright light flashed three times in the form of these words:

'**Go with the program. Go with the program. Go with the program.**'" God had given her the answer. I breathed a sigh of relief and said, "Thank you, Lord."

That very afternoon, Mom, Dad, and all four of us children sat again in the conference room at the hospital. When the doctor entered, he asked if she had made her decision; Mother didn't hesitate. "Yes, I will participate in the study program. Maybe I can eventually help someone else facing these same exact circumstances."

THE COMPUTER ASSIGNMENT

From there, the process took on a life of its own. We sat, waiting for the doctor to return, holding the computer assignment indicating how Mother would proceed in the program: Radiation or enucleation. "We have your assignment," he said, "Enucleation."

We sat silently after hearing this news. We secretly hoped the assignment would be radiation. Finally, I blurted out to the doctor, "Could you examine her eye one more time?"

He turned to Mother, and she nodded with approval. The doctor dilated her left eye, set up the instrument with the high-powered lens, turned to the family, and asked, "Would you like to look inside your Mother's eye? Sometimes, this helps the family."

One by one, we looked through the ophthalmoscope, the instrument that allowed us to see inside her eye. The cancerous tumor was attached to the inside eye membrane, hidden from the view of everyone else.

Mother's eye seemed so normal on the outside, yet something menacing was coiled inside like a venomous snake, watching for an opportunity to strike its prey.

One of the doctor's assistants explained, "A tumor like this starts out very small...somewhat like a freckle on the face. A single cell becomes irregular and starts multiplying.

STORY 9: Stomach in, Sternum high...

Your mother's tumor is medium-sized now."

The doctor broke in and surprised us when he announced, "I can schedule her surgery first thing in the morning." I wondered if he wanted to proceed quickly before she changed her mind. But Mother wasn't about to change her decision. She had heard from God!

WHAT'S IN THE BASKET?
In the wee hours of the following morning, our family, including two of mother's sisters, gathered to take Mother to surgery. The atmosphere was heavy and quiet. We didn't know what was up when Mother climbed into the van. She clutched a covered basket, holding it tightly like a hidden treasure. Dad got in behind her, carrying her suitcase. Everyone wondered, "What's in the basket?" But no one asked.

A few miles down the road, Mother unveiled what was hidden in her basket. It was a treasure. The moment she unwrapped it, the comforting aroma of Mother's kitchen filled the air.

"Here, thought you might be hungry," she announced with an upbeat voice as she placed a sausage biscuit in each outreached hand. We couldn't believe it, and yet, we could. Mother's spiritual bag had been packed many years ago, freeing her to think about feeding her family.

"Don't be worried about me," she tenderly said. "I looked in the mirror this morning, told my eye 'goodbye,' and thanked it for doing such a good job. Everything is going to be okay. God is with us."

THE REPORT
After the surgery, the doctor graced us with wonderful news: "The pathology reports look good, and we found no tumor extensions past her eye."

MORE ...
Mother was discharged from the hospital the following day, sporting a headband attached to her black eye patch. She was the prettiest female pirate we'd ever seen!

After four weeks of healing, we met with a highly recommended oculist in Atlanta, who would artfully create mother's "new" eye.

The Oculist discussed the procedure, took measurements, and evaluated the coloring in her right eye to ensure her new eye would be a perfect match.

On a bright day, the Oculist called with the news we'd been waiting for. "Your mother's eye prosthesis is ready." Even though we all arrived early, the Oculist immediately took Mother in. She invited us into the eye-fitting room and motioned for us to sit on a long sofa behind Mother.

All we could see was Mother's back and the Oculist's face as she sat across from Mother, leaning forward to begin her work. Minutes later, she handed Mother a mirror so she would be the first one to see herself.

A gasp of delight and an "Oh yes!" let us know Mother was pleased. Now, it was our turn. We couldn't wait to see the miracle for ourselves.

With her stomach in, sternum high, and shoulders back, Mother stood and turned to face her waiting audience. She flashed a big smile and winked with her beautiful new eye.

We all jumped to our feet, bursting with joy and applauding with delight, mingling with the sun's rays that danced around the room. Mother hugged each one of us, and last but not least, hugged and thanked the artistic Oculist.

Mother led the way out of the room, and I mentally placed my book in good posture on my head and followed behind her. I couldn't have loved her more than I did on that day. She was so tall in my eyes. Someone to proudly emulate.

It is this kind of influence that is passed down through

STORY 9: Stomach in, Sternum high...

generations. Mother, once again, showed us how to walk with faith and confidence, even when life's tapestry is temporarily woven with dark threads. She modeled a relationship with God that can never be shaken from its foundations. ~

*When she speaks, her words are wise,
and she gives instructions with kindness.*
(Proverbs 31:26 NLT)

STORY 10

Love Story, Part 1

The Joy of becoming Victorious after Failure

YOUNG LOVE, EARLY LIFE

I was born in Athens, GA, coming into the world as a chubby, red-faced baby girl. When Mother was pregnant with me, a well-meaning neighbor informed her, "I can tell by the way you are carrying your baby that it is a boy." So, of course, most of the baby clothes Mother bought were blue.

When I was about to make my debut, Mom and Dad rushed to the hospital, fully expecting to bring their firstborn, little "Jr." into the world. Did I ever surprise them?

All the little blue "Jr." clothes were exchanged for girlish pinks. My quite feminine Mother and macho Dad began the daunting task of raising me. Thus, my journey in the pursuit of "perfect womanhood" began. Occasionally, Mother commented, sometimes affectionately, and at other times with a "slight" edge in her voice, "Arlette, you came into this world equipped with a *very* strong self-will."

My first little brother came along three and a half years after I was born. I watched Mother take care of our new family addition and insisted that when he wailed, I just knew he "wanted to go back to the hospital."

After realizing that I didn't have the option of deciding whether or not I would be an only child, I settled into a pseudo-motherhood role and loved pretending to be "Mommy" when I played "house."

I pretended and announced with certainty that we had a chauffeur, and his name was Herbert. The significance of this name will make sense to you shortly. I was too young to know the "daddy" part of babies, so it was just my babies, me, and our chauffeur throughout my early years.

MR. RIGHT ...

One day, after reaching sixteen, I decided to pray about certain aspects of my future. Because my Mother's life revolved around taking me and, by now, my three siblings to church at least three times a week, I learned that I could pray about anything.

I once prayed for a husband, yet I told God I would be a missionary if that was His will for me. "Lord, if you need me in Africa, I'll go. If it's not Your plan for me to marry, that's okay, too. But just in case, if there is a 'Mr. Right,' please bring him into my life." God graciously answered my prayer three years later.

"Mr. Right" was handsomely gift-wrapped, and his name was Herbert Lavon Revells. The only problem, his first name was Herbert. Remember my imaginary chauffeur? I never thought I would end up marrying him!

Nonetheless, I quickly got over any objections. By the way, and much to my surprise, I later learned that "Herbert" means "general". I had no idea what was in store for me—neither did he. God matched the "General" and "Miss Strong Will." After dating a year, my knight in shining armor asked me to marry him.

The Sunday he asked my father for my hand in marriage was exciting indeed! We had opposite strengths, but both had strong wills. We were both firstborns and enjoyed the privilege of being raised in Christian homes. We wanted to do everything right and honor God in our relationship.

SETTLING INTO MARRIED LIFE

Our perfect and God-kissed wedding day arrived. Although our official honeymoon was short, because Lavon was still in college, we vowed that our honeymoon spirit would live on. I gladly put my academic career on hold for a while after attending Emmanuel College, and then I started attending The University of Georgia. However, when we married, I transferred from UGA to PHTS (Putting Hubby Through School).

I became pregnant with our first child during our first year of marriage. Close to the end of the eighth month of my pregnancy, the hospital staff at St. Mary's got to know us quite well.

Every time I had what I now know as Braxton Hicks contractions, I informed my on-alert husband, "This is IT." He rushed me to the hospital four times. Feel free to laugh with me here! It wasn't my fault, they never told me about Braxton Hicks contractions. We were so young and so uninformed.

On our fourth trip to the hospital, two weeks before the projected due date, the doctor decided to induce labor.

Forty hours later, my heart melted when I looked at the little face of our beautiful daughter, Laura Leigh. Her eyes were wide open, and she looked back at me as if to say, "We made it, Mom."

BACK TO WORK

After Laura was born, it was necessary for me to return to work. The only thing that gave me peace about leaving our newborn was that she was in the arms of the best caregiver I knew, my Mother.

Mother kept me informed about every level of development. One day, the phone rang, and I heard Mother's voice. She whispered, "Listen." I heard my baby girl laughing for the first time! I was excited to hear her first laugh, but warm tears rolled down my cheeks with sadness because I was not there.

Our darling second child came along during our second year of marriage. After waking up from the delivery (they put women to sleep back then), I asked for my baby. He was wrapped in a blue blanket. I took a peek and said, "Yep! You're a boy!" He was our adorable Christopher Lavon.

Everything seemed so perfect. We had a girl and a boy. By that time, Lavon had graduated with chemistry and biology degrees. Our plans for him were to go to graduate school. He insisted that he would get a temporary job first to help us get on our feet. That allowed me to stay at home with our babies. We were on a tight budget.

TWO BABIES

Even though we were not in the best financial shape to start a family, we excitedly welcomed our little blessings into our small, one-bedroom garage apartment. My young girl's dreams had all come true. "Mr. Right" was in my life, and I was now a real mommy—no more pretending! I absolutely loved taking our babies places. I relished motherhood. I never grew tired of hearing, "Your babies are so beautiful." Our little family had grown sooner than expected, but that felt okay.

None of us can imagine what is ahead. Tests of faith lurked around the corner, and we were about to come face to face with ours.

Love Story, Part 2
The Joy of God's Love Story

The Bible is God's Love Letter to us. He included accounts of people who failed miserably. However, in their lowest moments, God reached out to them in love. Here is how God's unconditional love reached me in my darkest moment.

Our two babies were taking bottles and in diapers (cloth, I might add) at the same time. I also took on typing projects, trying to supplement our family's finances. Playing house as a child was a lot easier. When I got tired, I put my baby dolls in their beds, set them on a shelf and walked away. Real life didn't work like that.

FINANCIAL ISSUES

We struggled so much financially, that we would be in deep trouble if we had not found a pharmacy that offered a charge account. This allowed us to buy the baby food and formula we needed.

While this helped significantly, we still experienced desperate times. One day, I called a small grocery store nearby and asked if I could open a grocery charge account. I explained our situation and the pleasant female voice on the other end of the phone said, "Yes, come on in."

Little Laurie and I raced to the store. She was just big enough to sit in the buggy seat of the grocery cart, so we strolled around the store. I was very pregnant with our second child.

I filled the grocery cart as high as I could with everything we needed. When I got to the checkout counter, I whispered to the man standing at the cash register that I had called earlier and was told I could charge the groceries now and pay later.

His face grew stern, and he said in a loud, abrupt voice, "No, we don't charge groceries here." I tried to stay calm and explained that I had already talked with someone on the phone. By now, people were curious about what was going on. My face was red. I felt humiliated, and no more words would come out.

The man behind the counter repeated himself. "I'm sorry, Ma'am, but we just don't accommodate customers charging food to a store account." I carefully lifted my baby from her perched position in the cart and ran for the door, leaving the cart full of groceries. I couldn't escape fast enough. Even now as I write this, I get worked up just thinking about it.

I know our parents would have been happy to help us financially, but my young groom felt he should take care of us. He was too proud to accept money from them. Neither of our parents had a clue that we were in such financial trouble.

ANOTHER PREGNANCY

Approximately a year later, I froze when the home pregnancy test showed I was pregnant again—so soon after our second

STORY 10: Love Story, Part 2

baby was born. My plan was to have four children—two close together, wait a few years, and then have two more. But it was much too soon for the "two more."

By the time Lavon got home from work that day, I was exhausted, desperate, and panicky, almost to the point of collapse. He saw it on my face and asked, "What's wrong?" I told him I had taken a home pregnancy test that day and it was positive. I immediately saw his own face grow tense.

I managed to get supper on the table and soon afterward tucked the little ones into bed for the night. We wanted to give our two children all the advantages we could. I joined Lavon in the living room to discuss our "situation." Then came our devastating decision.

The topic of abortion came up. It had just been legalized in New York. I remember saying, "It has got to be a legitimate option. For it to be legalized, it must mean that it is okay. After all, we do live in a Christian nation."

At that point, I was eight weeks pregnant. Lavon and I "chose" to believe that a person's spirit and soul enter the "mass of cells" when a baby takes his first breath at birth. That's when human life began, and abortion was another legal contraception—just another form of birth control. We chose abortion.

PLAN IN MOTION

We made travel plans. Others might have thought we were planning a "pleasure" trip. In our minds, we were simply taking advantage of the "medical advancements" that would make our lives "easier."

We knew our parents, and older folks we knew, wouldn't understand our progressive way of thinking, so we didn't discuss it with any of them. If only we had! We missed gaining wisdom and advice of trusted people. Instead, everyone assumed that I was accompanying my husband on a business trip, and we didn't correct them.

NEW YORK CITY

We arrived safely in New York City. Snow covered the ground. The taxi driver drove much too fast for me from the airport to our downtown hotel. You just don't drive that fast in snow, at least not back home in Georgia. I didn't say anything that made me look afraid.

Truth be told, I didn't tell Lavon about a terrible gnawing feeling that kept returning. I *was* afraid! I know now that he was hiding his own misgivings. I reached for my husband's hand as we silently stared forward from the back of the cab.

THE CLINIC

The next morning, we awakened early, dressed, and found the clinic just before our 9 am appointment. When we walked in the door of the small waiting area, I saw a teenage girl sitting on a sofa next to her mother. The mom's arm was draped across the girl's shoulders. Both their heads dropped when we walked in.

My first thought, "How sad. That beautiful young teenager must have gotten pregnant out of wedlock." I was so grateful that my situation was different; I was married. I was in a respectable, committed relationship. (Looking back, I'm shocked that I thought abortion was wrong for her, but not for me!) I checked in at the reception desk, sat down by my husband, and waited. My turn came. Lavon squeezed my hand as I stood to walk into the procedure room.

Thirty minutes later, I came back out. Lavon asked, "Are you alright, honey?" Many years later, I asked Lavon how he felt while I was in the procedure room. He said, "I looked around and felt spiritual darkness in the waiting room, but I had mixed feelings. I was anxious and also relieved, but that didn't last long. When I saw you walk out with your pale face

STORY 10: Love Story, Part 2

and trembling body, a foreboding, depressive feeling washed over me. I knew instantly we had made a horrible mistake."

In an effort to move on with our lives and put what we had done in the past, that afternoon we toured the city, ate at a nice restaurant, and attended a Broadway play that evening.

TWO DOORS

The next morning, we boarded the flight to Atlanta, picked up our luggage, and walked out of the airport. I can still hear the click of the heavy glass exit door as it closed behind us.

Simultaneously, another door clicked shut inside me, the door to my inner prison. This would be the place where my deep, dark secret lived. With time, it became such a familiar part of me that I didn't realize it even existed.

INTERNAL PRISON

We continued on with our lives, relieved that we had made it possible to have a fresh start. It was as if our trip to New York City never happened. Not a word was spoken between Lavon and me about our morning at the clinic. We allowed the feeling of relief to take precedence over any other feelings.

I avoided all the information that had begun to emerge about the abortion issue. I determined that no one was going to make me feel like I had done anything wrong. I had a "mass of cells" removed. That's it. End of story.

SURFACING OF THE DEEP SECRET

One Sunday morning, ten years later, it happened—my world crashed. Lavon and I were both very active in the church. I served as the president of Women's Ministries, taught Sunday School, and played the piano. Lavon was a deacon, Men's Fellowship President, and also a Sunday School teacher.

A high school friend visited our church that Sunday morning. I had not seen him since he left to go to medical college after graduating high school. After I introduced my friend to Lavon, my friend asked, "How many children do you have?"

Suddenly, my subconscious woke up. From my deepest place, I blurted out the truth I had been hiding for ten years. "We have three children." Lavon looked at me strangely and quickly said, "We have two children."

"No," I persisted, "We have three."

Uneasy about what was happening, Lavon, put his arm around me and pulled me close. He made a final remark before excusing us from the conversation. "We have only two children, but sometimes it seems like three," he said as he put his arm around my waist and walked me to the car. At that moment, I felt like the ground was falling out from under my feet—like I was falling into a bottomless pit.

I realized that I had been forcing an "inflated volleyball" of pain and guilt under the "water" for a long time and had run out of strength to keep it submerged any longer. The intense pressure from the deep explosively forced my submerged feelings to the surface.

When we got into the car, I began weeping and mourning with such agony that it scared Lavon. I cried for days. No one could help me. No one human, that is. Some years later, Lavon shared that he was grieving, too. He said, "I had a dream about our baby not long after our trip to New York City. It was a boy."

I knew the guilt and agony of how Peter must have felt after denying that he knew Christ. Scripture tells us that he went outside and wept bitterly. My grief was so consuming that when I was alone, I also "wept bitterly." I knew I deserved the agony I was feeling, but it soon reached a breaking point.

HELPLESS

Time went on, but my life was anything but normal. Not only

STORY 10: Love Story, Part 2

did I choose to keep what I had done a secret, I kept my pain private as well. When I was alone, I sobbed uncontrollably. Because of shame, I "hid" from God and didn't know how to pray.

God saw my heart and knew that I was in a bottomless pit of grief, in a prison of self-hatred and unforgiveness. I didn't know how to reach up. God knew what He had to do—He reached down for me! It happened a couple of weeks after we encountered our friend at church.

HOLY AWARENESS MOMENT

I was alone in my car. Miserable. Suddenly, I yelled out, "Jesus, help me!" God's Spirit enveloped me with compassion, and He gently said, "Give Me your empty blanket."

I suddenly stopped sobbing. It had never occurred to me that I was, in essence, carrying around an empty blanket. I reached up with my right hand and cried as loudly as I could, "Here, God. Here's my empty blanket!" I sensed His hand reach down, taking the empty blanket as I lifted it up to Him. An assurance flooded me. Our baby was with Him in Heaven. Perhaps Jesus rocked our son in that very blanket and sang the lullabies I would have sung if I'd rocked him in my own arms. My life came full circle amid God's mercy.

Thus, God opened the door of my internal prison, and the healing process began. In the words of a friend, Chuck Pierce, "The hovering power of the Spirit of God, and the speaking Voice of our Creative Lord, can break any power of chaos around us, and create new order out of our confusion."

The Creative Lord spoke into my life and broke the power of chaos caused by my past actions. It was a life-changing experience. He set my world in Kingdom order. I saw firsthand the power of Kingdom life in action; a testament to God answering Jesus' prayer: "Thy Kingdom come. Thy will be done."

I could relate to the blind beggar in Mark 10, Bartimaeus, who was sitting beside the roadside begging. Scripture tells us that when he heard that Jesus was passing by, he began shouting, "Jesus, Son of David, have mercy on me!" Many people in the passing crowd rebuked the blind beggar and told him to be quiet; nevertheless, he shouted even more, "Jesus, Son of David, have mercy on me!"

Jesus stopped and said, "Call him."

People who heard Jesus started calling out to the blind man, "Cheer up! On your feet! He's calling you." Throwing his cloak aside, he jumped to his feet and came to Jesus.

When Jesus asked the blind man, "What do you want me to do for you?" The blind man said, "Rabbi, I want to see."

Jesus told him, "Go, your faith has healed you." Immediately, the blind man received his sight and followed Jesus along the road.

UNCONDITIONAL LOVE

I'm absolutely convinced there is nothing that can keep us away from God's unconditional love!

> "Neither height nor depth nor anything else in all creation will be able to separate us from the love of God that is in Christ Jesus our Lord (Romans 8:39)."

What event is hidden in your prison of shame? What are you spending all your energy on to keep out of sight, submerged beneath the surface of the waters? Reading my story, you perhaps realized that you are also out of strength. You've lived with your secret pain long enough; today is the day to change that. Our past is not our future.

Maybe in reading about the beautiful way God reached out to me, you realized the compassionate nature of God, who forgives, redeems, and offers new life. He delivers those He loves from the bottomless pit. He is the lifter of our heads. His gaze melts all shame. Dare to cry out! Look up. He's waiting with open arms. "He brought me out into a spacious place; he rescued me because he delighted in me (Psalm 18:19)."

MORE ...
God can take an ordinary person and do extraordinary things through us. First, God does something in us and then through us.

People started coming into my life who continued to help in the healing process. I was at a business dinner and "happened" to be seated at the same table with a lovely lady named Pat. During the course of the evening, she asked me what type of business I was in and then told me she was the director of a local pregnancy center. I'm not sure if my intense interest prompted her, but she asked if I would like to volunteer some of my time to help at the center. Lavon and I still guarded our secret, but I was beginning to feel a strong desire to reach out and help other women.

Since I owned a business, my time was limited, but I found a couple of hours a week that I could volunteer at the pregnancy center. God had shown me His love and compassion, and I wanted to extend that same love and compassion to others.

I've often wondered about that young girl who shared the clinic waiting room with me that day in 1970. What has her life been like since then? I pray for her. Perhaps, if she hasn't found peace with herself and God, she may even read this book and allow God to do what He has done for me.

During a conversation with a gynecologist friend, I shared my experience of having undergone abortion and how I am passionate about helping others who have made the same decision. He responded by saying, "I have always believed that every woman who has had an abortion will have to face it someday."

VICTORIOUS AFTER FAILURE

God is compassionately reaching out to you and me. He wants to free us from those things that keep us from running towards His will for our lives. Do you want to be set free? God wants to do it—He longs to do it. Friend, you can be victorious after failure.

The first step is to give your empty blanket to God. Just wait and see what He does with it. He may fill your blanket with the gift of allowing a baby's adoption to a childless person or couple. Or the gift of reaching out for help with your emotional or mental needs. Or the gift of a broken relationship needing forgiveness. Or the gift of self-forgiveness and freedom from whatever prison you are in.

He is waiting. ~

POST NOTE

God does not ask everyone to share their painful experiences publicly, but He confirmed this was His plan for me when He gave me this vision. I saw a collapsed bridge, the weight of it crushed layer upon layer of vehicles beneath it. He said, "I will reach many crushed hearts through you."

I pray the Holy Awareness Moment stories in this book bring you comfort and inspiration.

All the glory belongs to our loving Father!

He reached down from on high
and took hold of me;
He pulled me out of deep water.
(Psalm 18:16)

EPILOGUE

Lavon completed his formal education with distinction and has built a successful career in chemistry. His dedication and hard work have earned him numerous accolades, including several achievement awards at regional and national levels.

Arlette has completed her first book.

Our journey has certainly had its ups and downs. Still, we feel incredibly blessed by the love and support we've received from God and our family. Our daughter Laura is married to the wonderful Greg, and our son Christopher has found his happily ever after with Jeannie. They have brought us joy and given us thirteen amazing grandchildren, bringing happiness and laughter into our lives. We are thrilled to have a new granddaughter through the marriage of our grandson, Brennan. Through their love our first great-grandchild, Mason, was born. We are just so grateful for everything we have, and we feel blessed to have each other and the love of God in our lives.

*Yours, Lord, is the greatness and the power
and the glory and the majesty and the splendor,
for everything in heaven and earth is Yours.
Yours, Lord, is the kingdom;
You are exalted as head over all.
Now, our God, we give you thanks,
and praise your glorious name.*

(Prayer of King David in 1 Chronicles 29:11,13)

Lavon & Arlette

Laura and her husband, Greg

Christopher and his wife, Jeannie

Lavon with our 6 grandsons: (back row) David, John-James, Lavon, Chase, Brennan, (front row) Garrett and Andrew, (inset) Brennan & Katie

Arlette with our 7 granddaughters: (back row) Elysiana, Gabriella, Olivia, Arlette, Victoria, Isabella, (front row) Sophia and Havah

ABOUT THE AUTHOR

Arlette Revells . . . is a talented artist and the founder of Great Works Creation Company. Her book, *Joys of the Not So Perfect Woman: Stories of Holy Awareness Moments with a Perfect God*, is filled with heartwarming stories presented in an entertaining and relatable manner. Women who have heard her speak praise her outstanding communication skills and how she never fails to make them laugh.

Her commitment to making a difference in her community is evident in her numerous roles. She was honored as the Woman of the Year in 2017 by Hugh's News, a testament to her significant contributions. For several years, she has ministered through Joysprings Foundation, Inc., a ministry that provides Times of Refreshment for ministry leaders. She serves on the executive board of VOHSC - Violins of Hope South Carolina, highlighting her dedication to the arts.

Arlette's personal life is a testament to her ability to balance her professional and personal responsibilities. She has been happily married to Lavon, a chemist, for over 55 years. In her eyes, Lavon is still her knight in shining armor. Together, they have raised two children who married incredible mates, adding to their joy as grandparents to thirteen grandchildren. Their family has recently expanded with the addition of a lovely bonus granddaughter, who married one of their six grandsons.

Arlette's life experiences as a wife, mother, grandmother (a.k.a. GiGi), friend, author, inspirational storyteller, and business owner have made her relevant, insightful, and unforgettable.

www.ArletteRevells.com

www.ingramcontent.com/pod-product-compliance
Lightning Source LLC
Chambersburg PA
CBHW071147090426
42736CB00012B/2263